ROGER L. PICKAR

◆◆◆◆◆◆◆◆◆◆◆◆◆◆◆◆

# MARKETING FOR DESIGN FIRMS IN THE 1990s

◆◆◆◆◆◆◆◆◆◆◆◆◆◆◆◆

The American Institute of Architects Press
Washington, D.C.

*To the inspirations of my life — Gloria, my late Mom, Dad,*
*brother Ken, and my girls—*
*Amy, Julie, and Sarah*

The American Institute of Architects Press
1735 New York Avenue, N.W.
Washington, D.C. 20006


Library of Congress Cataloging-in-Publication Data

Pickar, Roger L.
       Marketing for design firms in the 1990s / Roger L. Pickar
             p.       cm.
       ISBN 1-55835-037-3
       1. Architectural services marketing—United States    I. Title.
NA1996.P5     1991
750 ' .68 ' 8—dc20                                     91-13386
                                                       CIP


Designed by Mosser Design Inc, Washington, D.C.
Edited by Pamela James Blumgart

# Contents

# PREFACE

◆◆◆◆◆◆◆◆◆◆◆◆◆◆◆

## THE '90s:
VARIOUS
TRENDS AND
REACTIONS

I n the 1990s changing needs and shifting economic conditions will force everyone to market smarter or perish. A declining or shrinking mature market requires business strategies based on solid information about what can save, or damage, a firm's economic future. Survival and success will depend on a company's ability to adapt to trends in the marketplace and to gain solid, current information from narrowly focused markets. Successful firms will also engage in good, flexible, strategic thinking about what they should be doing and what marketing strategies will meet these goals.

## The wave of the future

The old, technically driven firms of the '70s and '80s will find it difficult to compete in '90s markets. These companies attend to many different types of clients and buildings and ask the question, "This is who we are; who needs us?" Market-driven firms tend to market fewer building types and make the announcement, "Here is the need, and yes, we can fill it." In the '90s firms will have to fit themselves to the market in order to survive.

To find a niche in the marketplace of the '90s, firms must have marketing programs that take a proactive stance, that is, that prepare to acquire the client before the client has a specific project in mind. In the '80s it was very common for firms to take on a marketing program, and many achieved a better number of projects as a result. However, as the marketing gospel has spread, more firms have moved from reactive marketing (waiting for a project announcement) to proactive marketing (approaching the client before a project is announced). In the '90s progressive firms will move further, to preemptive marketing (offering solutions to the earliest problems a potential client may have).

Firms that increasingly take a market-oriented stance will significantly reduce their reactive jobs—those acquired by competing and winning in high-profile, highly competitive reactive situations. In the '90s marketing sophisticates will outmaneuver local reactive firms and even proactive locals by getting to potential clients with earlier solutions. Firms sophisticated in marketing will be more specialized in the types of facilities their prospective clients want, making them better able to speak the language of a particular client.

Instituting such preemptive marketing requires that a firm redefine its business in order to gain the allegiance of prospective buyers at the earliest point possible in their decision-making process. This market-driven approach often takes a firm out of the normal definition of what architect/engineers, land planners, or interior designer/architects would call their business. However, most firms that attack the market in this manner will become increasingly self-sufficient. By getting there early and becoming involved with the first problem a potential client has, market-driven firms can preempt the competition as the client moves to the contractual stages.

As more firms begin to recognize the value of reaching the client early and the advantages of not depending on the local economy, the '90s will see many firms evolve from generalists to specialists. These specialists will become increasingly sensitive to the needs of their prospective clients and those clients' clients. Because of their experience, these design firms will be willing to commit more than the generalists can in terms of promises and follow-through. With good radar and market research these firms will often take a project off the market before the local generalists even hear about it, leaving the impression that "there is just less work out there."

To have the best chance of being one of the firms culling the work early, a design firm must fit itself for several specific markets and engage in tactics that make it the obvious choice for design buyers in those markets. One advantage market-driven firms have is their ability to move out of their own local base. In contrast to the technically driven firm, which is generally unable to succeed in the competition outside its own market, market-driven firms that expand geographically will have more flexibility to help them meet turbulent times.

To keep clients once they have been snared, design firms must take a further step. Market Research Service's many studies show that more than two-thirds of the companies buying design are looking for a significant improvement in the level of service they are offered. This emphasis on service will grow in the '90s. Bombarded by sophisticated, consumer-oriented approaches from outside the industry, design buyers will become even more demanding consumers. The "nadering" of the public and the aging of a generation that has embraced consumerism will make the decade ripe for firms that can respond to the most demanding clients.

Designers have commonly gone to school to learn design, and schools have not trained them in customer service. However, as companies become increasingly driven by the markets they want to attract, their emphasis on client service will have to grow. Design- or product-oriented firms that do not focus on the key issue of customer service will find this a major stumbling block to achieving even basic marketing goals.

---

# What a good marketing plan can do

Ever-changing markets, less explosive growth, and increasingly more demanding clients in the '90s require the development of responsive, workable marketing programs. A simple, flexible system of marketing planning will allow smaller companies with limited time and personnel to develop and use a marketing plan efficiently.

Although many books have been written on marketing and strategic/tactical planning, most of these assume that all companies either have many employees to perform the required tasks or that these companies have developed and implemented strategic plans in the past. This book, however, will present a fast-track and more flexible planning program for the '90s and for firms initiating a marketing planning process or trying to improve their process with limited resources.

It is designed to provide architects, engineers, landscape architects,

> ### Four Observations Critical to Marketing for the '90s
>
> ◇ Knowing your clients also means understanding their business.
> ◇ No two prospects will have identical demands. Clients will become more differentiated and decentralized.
> ◇ Trying to plan for more than three years will be increasingly difficult. Economic, social, and political events will move as fast as or faster than they did in the last decade.
> ◇ Flexibility and responsiveness to market changes will be the two rules of survival.

and other designers with a fairly simple, step-by-step marketing planning process. The objective is to alleviate, even eliminate, the pain of creating or improving a marketing program. In fact, I hope this book can turn your initial apprehension about marketing into a rewarding and exciting experience. The methods discussed are easy to understand, motivational, and simple to implement.

Three ingredients are needed for a company to achieve a successful marketing program:

- ◆ An effective work force, including a person dedicated to coordinating the marketing effort
- ◆ Development of a step-by-step plan and an established schedule for its implementation
- ◆ A genuine commitment to forge ahead even after mistakes are made

With these in place, a good, well-implemented marketing plan will achieve any or all of the common objectives: more work, a better mix of work, increased fees, and a consistent workload.

# 1

◆◆◆◆◆◆◆◆◆◆◆◆◆◆

THE
MARKETING
APPROACH
THAT REALLY
WORKS

Rapid, uncontrolled growth, especially in areas of limited experience, can be frightening for a company. It can cause sporadic losses in quality, which in turn can damage the hard-won business on which a company depends. A sales dip on a short-term basis can be equally damaging, leading to layoffs or to overstaffing, which is demoralizing and costly in terms of profitability. Debts incurred in healthier times can also threaten a company's survival.

A successful marketing program can stabilize your company's job base and help you survive tough economic times. One way of looking at marketing has proved particularly effective for design firms. This chapter will outline this proactive approach, which is the basis for the marketing planning process as it is explained in the rest of this book.

## Design firms' marketing problems

In 1988 Market Research Services of Longwood, Florida, conducted a survey of 188 companies to ascertain why certain design firms beat the competition in getting contracts. Some clear decision-making patterns emerged that revealed a distinct change from previous patterns. In particular, the primary criterion design buyers used in choosing a company had become trustworthiness. As one firm's president said, "Trust is the No. 1 ingredient" in selecting professional architects, engineers, planners, and landscape architects. Eighty-eight percent of those surveyed agreed.

According to participants in the study, the following criteria were also important in their selection process:
- the ability to get the job done on time (56 percent)
- the ability to get the job done within budget (53 percent)
- the technical experience to get the job done efficiently and competently (41 percent)

The importance of technical experience averaged a high 74 percent among respondents dealing with complex building types such as hospitals and high-tech facilities. Design buyers in the public sector were also particularly concerned with this factor. Facilities managers, elected officials, and engineers hoped to avoid constructing a building that would sprout deficiencies in two to five years and, as a result, all rated technical competence highly.

Still, the consideration consistently cited by all decision-makers was trustworthiness.

In a 1988 survey Market Research Services asked forty-seven design firms why they had lost prospective clients and contracts for which they had had serious hopes. Specifically, the survey asked which contracts had been lost the previous year and how the design firms would characterize the reasons for losing them. Each firm was asked to list ten jobs.

Although firms operating in the private sector offered many reasons for failing to get the jobs, 82 percent of the contracts were lost to competitors "who got there first." This figure was lower in the public sector, but a surprising 21 percent of this traditionally competitive sector also lost out for this reason.

In a 1989 study of twenty-eight design firms, Market Research Services posed a simple question: "Are you selling quality, service, or product?" In 71 percent of the cases, the firm's project managers answered "quality." Five ongoing clients of each participating firm were then asked, "What is the most important reason for doing business with X firm?" The reply in 76 percent of the cases was that service was the most important factor. Quality was a support factor only 26 percent of the time. Almost all said fair pricing was critical.

In our interviews of the design firms, certain facts became apparent:

♦ Over a span of years (usually more than five) the firm had developed a "better and better product."

♦ The quality of this product was exceedingly important to the design firm and its staff; quality was considered part of the company's identity or culture. More often than not the group took particular pleasure in delineating the special things they added to their projects. Quality had become the vehicle for recognition and gratification within the group.

♦ The design firms were not certain how essential this improved product was to their clients. Staff and principals had rarely asked clients if these quality features were understood or appreciated.

In their interviews, 65 percent of the design buyers stated they had actually assumed reasonable quality, but that over a period of time the need for a high level of service had become even more important.

In a 1990 Market Research Services study of fifty-seven design firms with $3.0 million to $6.2 million in fee volume, we found that most presidents or partners in charge did not truly believe they were in control of their firms' growth. A review of their companies' growth histories revealed that 70 percent had marketed reactively, that is, depended on the marketplace to dictate where, when, how, and if the company would grow. In rapidly growing specialty or vertical markets, many reactive firms were successful until work in the market or geographic area leveled off or declined. In areas or markets with no growth or slow growth, success depended on the management team's ability to sell reactively and to manage crises. Although many of these firms were moderately successful, owners often told of losing the most profitable jobs and 70 percent of them believed a little more knowledge of marketing techniques would have made their firms considerably more profitable. With a recession approaching, many of these firms were scurrying to become proactive and abandon their now untenable reactionary position.

As these studies show, certain interconnected factors emerge as problem areas for design firms that look for jobs solely by reacting to the market. Decision-makers often prefer to hire companies they already know and trust, that will offer them good service and respond specifically to their concerns. Such firms usually behave proactively—that is, engage in activities that introduce them to prospective clients early in the decision-making process and give them the opportunity to establish a trusting relationship with those prospects. This relationship sets up an early view of their companies as firms that offer good service. We'll talk about these concepts in more detail below.

Before we go any further, let's take a look at how your prospective clients choose a design firm. Almost all clients make decisions by going through a basic process that could be called "Think, Announce, Award." In the Think Phase, the design buyer sifts and evaluates past experiences, current opportunities, and potential future projects to help decide whether to proceed. In the Announce Phase the decision-maker or a subordinate initiates the tasks necessary to bring the project to fruition. At this point, the company begins to use outside services, although there may be no formal announcement. Individual support services (such as surveying or geotechnical engineering) are selected stage by stage. The Announce Phase is best characterized by the prospect's decision to "go" with the project, although it still could fall apart for reasons of feasibility or financing. For the design firm, the Award Phase is the moment of truth when the decision-maker signs a contract and you find out whether your marketing strategy has worked.

## The wrong stuff

Firms in Market Research Services' studies that were dissatisfied with their marketing efforts had two elements in common: They regarded what they had to offer from a technical angle and they used a reactive, sales approach to looking for work.

Selling in a very competitive environment requires a technically driven, sales-oriented firm to identify where the work is, introduce its work to the prospective client, submit proposals when necessary, and improve the firm's chances of being on the final, select list. In this environment the marketing process is accelerated, allowing only a brief time in which to establish the firm's competence. In this often price-sensitive situation, buyers see most design firms as equal, and often low price and politics supplant professionalism and competence as reasons for hiring a designer.

Such technically driven firms operate from a sales rather than a marketing outlook. Typically they place themselves at the center of their marketing strategies, offering the same resources to many markets. This means they are not as knowledgeable in specific markets as their more focused, market-driven competitors. They leave lead generation until late in the prospective client's decision-making process, when the competition is greater. They depend on salespeople knocking on doors, reacting to some targeted and many untargeted leads, screening these, bringing in "the team," and eventually bringing some prospects to contract. Their success depends almost totally on the business development principal or specialist's ability to identify, screen, and sell to large numbers of prospects.

The stages of the sales approach are listed here:

- Making direct cold calls
- Advertising and networking with contacts to identify prospects
- Screening leads for potential through direct contact (telephone/visit) by a company representative
- Sending out or presenting brochures or support materials to prospective clients (Sometimes this is done before the screening step.)
- Making sales contacts (Some prospects drop out here for reasons such as lack of financing or zoning approval.)
- Bringing the client to contract, either through bidding or negotiation

The sales approach usually does not have specific targets and strategies. Although it is sometimes able to generate negotiated work in the private sector, its lack of focus results in a high cost-per-sales ratio because so many prospects must be identified and screened through cold calls.

Disadvantages of functioning as a technically driven, reactive marketer include the following:

- These firms are rarely perceived as experts in their own geographic marketplace. Moreover, out-of-town experts often skim the cream off their markets.
- Their profitability is reduced because they must constantly start work from scratch in different markets.
- They often merely react to the marketplace because they do not have experts able to identify potential clients early in the planning process or to stay in touch with the long-term problems of the market.
- They have a harder time negotiating as they often cannot offer expertise to save clients time and money.
- Often they are affected by short and mid-term ups and downs in the market because they have no specialty in which they are so expert they can overwhelm the competition.

# Sales Approach

1. Generate & Identify Prospects

2. Screening

3. Brochures/support materials

4. Sales contacts

5. Sales closing (bid or negotiate)

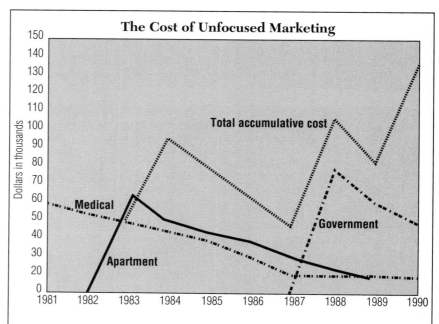

**The Cost of Unfocused Marketing**

This graph demonstrates the hidden costs associated with frequent changes in a firm's targeted markets. Over a three-year period, the hypothetical firm entered a new market each year—apartment, medical, and government. In each case the firm had to restructure its production and marketing efforts. Then, before the staff had mastered the skills of production and marketing for the new market, the firm entered another new market. This uncontrolled expansion led to high costs, lower-than-anticipated margins, and an increased risk of failure. The result was an annual increase in the cost of doing business, represented by the total accumulative cost line in this chart.

To refine and improve your firm's existing skills and to market to firms with projects in your area of expertise is much less costly and meets the challenge of change without demanding an unreasonable investment of time and money.

As a result of their sales-oriented practices, reactive marketers spend too much time on clients and jobs that are too small, too competitive, or outside their firms' operational and marketing experience. The approach causes a number of other problems as well:

- ◆ It is expensive in terms of the number of estimates, presentations, and sales calls involved.
- ◆ This approach offers a shorter-term view of what the workload will be in a few months.
- ◆ It sometimes makes it necessary to take any job that is available.

Some factors may make functioning as a reactive, technically driven firm seem advantageous:

- ◆ It requires little change or investment.

- As long as there is a lot of work in the marketplace, it provides some profitability.
- It works fast.
- It feels simple and comfortable; no habits have to be broken.
- It requires less marketing.
- It reduces the risk of investing time and money in a project that doesn't go.

Typically, all that is required for reactive marketing is a brochure, a statement of qualifications, and a brief presentation. In some technical situations, extensive presentations may be necessary to become prequalified. For firms that acquire jobs only by responding to requests for public competition or bids, the simpler, reactive approach to marketing may suffice. However, by the time a firm reacts at the Announce Phase, it is usually too late to negotiate because a proactive competitor has already secured the job. Firms that want to be on selected short lists will find it helpful to abandon the reactive approach and exercise the proactive approach to marketing, while those that want to negotiate for work will find it essential.

## The right stuff

More effective in obtaining negotiated work than the reactive, technically driven sales approach is the proactive, market-driven marketing approach. It reaches clients and potential clients earlier in their decision-making process, at the Think Phase, and gains their trust by focusing salespeople on key issues. A design firm marketing in this way tries to provide its prospective clients with data about design issues of particular concern to those prospects. Accompanying this critical information with company literature can give your firm a foot in the door. Following up your initial contact by continuing to make such information available develops the potential client's trust and increases the likelihood of bringing that company to contract. Marketing in a negotiated environment takes time and interaction. The earlier a marketing program strikes at a prospect, the more time there is to demonstrate the elements of trustworthiness—dependability, honesty, integrity, consistency, and expertise. Despite this investment of time, the costs and results of this approach make for a much greater return on investment than your firm can get from using the reactive, sales approach.

The stages involved in this proactive approach to marketing are
- Agreeing to focus on particular markets and client types
- Researching the markets, generating leads, and networking to identify and screen prospects and their needs and attitudes
- Determining what the buyer wants, then developing promotional material and tailoring your presentation to fit
- Closing the contract through the development of trust and the

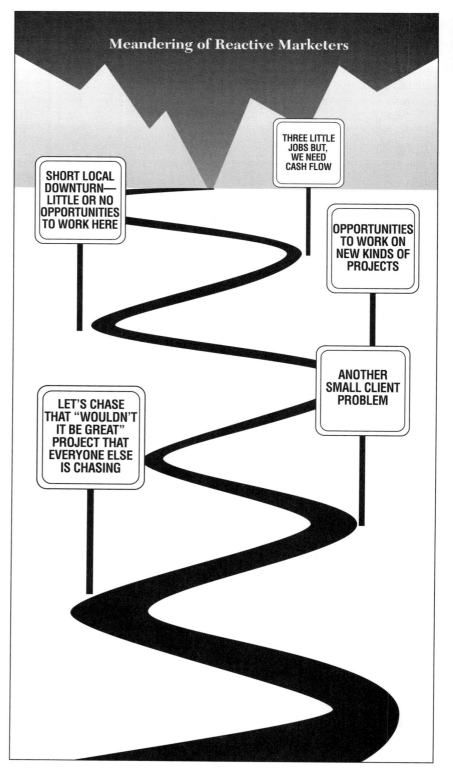

Meandering of Reactive Marketers

THREE LITTLE JOBS BUT, WE NEED CASH FLOW

SHORT LOCAL DOWNTURN— LITTLE OR NO OPPORTUNITIES TO WORK HERE

OPPORTUNITIES TO WORK ON NEW KINDS OF PROJECTS

ANOTHER SMALL CLIENT PROBLEM

LET'S CHASE THAT "WOULDN'T IT BE GREAT" PROJECT THAT EVERYONE ELSE IS CHASING establishment of a relationship as a competent provider of industry information.

Unlike technically driven firms, market-driven firms research and select their markets and niches carefully. They choose a market that has a deep need and surround it with dedicated resources. The majority of the firm's services—including marketing, administration, and finance operations—are integrated to create a deeper understanding of and sensitivity to the market's needs, idiosyncrasies, and trends.

Market-driven firms understand the important concerns in the types of projects potential clients engage in and impart objective information helpful in dealing with those concerns. (For example, if a prospect has complained about leaky roofs, these firms offer practical advice about roof design.) Providing such information as a means of gaining the prospect's trust can be called soft selling, in contrast to the aggressive, self-centered hard sell in which designers tell clients what design services they provide and how badly the clients need them.

Many successful proactive marketers have a system for addressing the first thoughts of a potential client that makes them so indispensable their strategy is really preemptive. Once you have bonded with a client in this earliest phase, it is difficult for a competitor to come in and take the project away from your firm.

Some advantages and disadvantages of employing this method of marketing are listed here. The deep expertise of proactive, market-driven firms allows them to

- save start-up time.
- take a longer term view of opportunities in the market.
- penetrate the market by identifying potential clients more easily.
- sell work more easily because the firm has a sense of the prospective clients' potential problems.

Other advantages of using this approach include these:

- It allows you to establish your firm's uniqueness.
- It diminishes the importance of price in the design selection process.

There are also some difficulties involved in proactive marketing:

- The approach takes time to develop.
- It takes discipline, commitment, and support from management.
- A considerable amount of research is needed to understand each market.
- It extends the time between initial contact and close of sale.
- The first couple of projects in a specific market require a lot of extra work because of the firm's lack of experience in that market.

◆ It doesn't guarantee success. Despite considerable invested time, some projects will still not come to fruition.

To summarize, market-driven firms of the '90s will have deeper experience in fewer markets. They will service a few markets better than their technically driven counterparts, which tend to react to many circumstances and repeatedly work with many different types of clients and building types without benefit of in-depth experience.

## What it takes to market proactively

How do you take a reactive firm and convert it into a proactive firm, one ahead of the marketplace and in control of its growth? How can your company grow smoothly and control its growth at a desired rate? Options for managing growth are complex, but Market Research Services's studies have yielded some characteristics that are common to firms that market proactively or preemptively:

◆ Proactive firms understand who they are, where they are exceptional and where they are mediocre, and how and when they perform well and poorly. They understand their resources and their limitations, in finances as well as talent.

◆ Proactive firms truly understand their markets and prospective clients before and better than the competition.

◆ Proactive firms have superior knowledge and firm-wide sensitivity to the needs and concerns of clients and prospects and the trends that will affect those needs.

◆ Proactive firms have a consistent system for extracting early prospective client and job type information from the market place before the competition.

◆ Proactive firms know the depth of potential in each market segment, understand complaints from the prospect's past as well as changes about to take place, and attack them before the competition.

◆ Proactive firms understand the competition's strengths and weaknesses as well as its history in challenging certain market places. In sum, the equation for proactive services is **Knowledge of the earliest prospective client decisions + a system for reaching them + sensitivity, commitment, and understanding of prospects' needs = proactive marketing.**

In a 1987 survey of Market Research Services' clientele, I found most of my clients were either waiting for prospects to show some manifestation of a decision about to be made or marketing to specific situations rather than prospects. A minority (26 percent) were marketing to prospects in the Think Phase and an even smaller minority (6 percent) were marketing to prospects before the Think Phase. Twenty-six firms in the study had chosen to move into a new marketplace (geographic or specialty) without assessing the strength of the competition or what it would take to accomplish a reasonable, achievable market share. By their own admission they were disappointed, sometimes deeply, with their results. An understanding of the equation for proactive marketing would have helped these design firms make reasonable, calculated decisions to help them reach their growth or profitability objectives.

Steps for developing and implementing a proactive marketing approach are presented in chapters 2 through 6 of this book. The remainder of this chapter will cover some tips for developing rapport with your prospects and supplying good service to keep them once they've become your clients.

## Suggestions for establishing trust

First, you must recognize that trustworthiness is not a product to sell. Rather, it is a perception one person develops of another based on the way that person acts or behaves. You create trust by exhibiting the qualities of being trustworthy. For example, Walter Cronkite never said, "You can trust me. I know the answers." He developed a trusting relationship with the American public by demonstrating trustworthy behavior over a long period. In fact, one of the elements that deeply concerned CBS executives about Cronkite's successor was his ability to inspire trust. Dan Rather was more intense, often asking probing, aggressive, straightforward questions of trusted public officials. His behavior did not inspire trust, but subtly evoked the public's awe and concern.

What, then, are the elements of trust? A good combination of the characteristics that follow will help individual members of your firm display trustworthiness.

**Communication patterns**. Prospects more often than not like to talk about their problems and have them heard. People who listen well and ask pertinent questions demonstrate trustworthiness. As a design firm representative approaching potential clients, prepare open-ended, nonaggressive questions prospects will feel comfortable answering. Their responses to these questions should reveal their concerns. If not, continue to ask questions until you have found a "hot button" or, preferably, many "hot buttons."

In addition to attentive listening, offer prospective clients informative verbal communication. Don't be too fast with answers. Slow, well-thought-out speech is associated with trustworthiness. People who speak too rapidly are thought to be "sales pitching" and not carefully thinking about their words. Talking too quickly and too much also suggests you are more concerned with yourself than with your prospective client.

**Positive self-image**. Displaying a favorable self-image to a prospective client can be tricky. You don't want to underestimate your abilities, but you don't want to sound as if you're bragging. Give a straightforward but honest profile of your company. List accomplishments as noted by others, and avoid extravagant claims such as "We're the most service-oriented firm in the state." Even if you think it's true, state it as a goal: "Our goal is to be the most service-oriented firm in the state."

Center your conversation on providing information that meets the prospective client's needs. Don't make the job sound simple. People trust those who recognize the complexity of accomplishing hard tasks and who respond with well-thought-out answers balanced by enthusiasm and commitment.

Above all, never talk negatively about the competition. Discussing a competitor's unethical behavior, lack of integrity, or dishonesty with a prospective client is in bad taste and reflects poorly on you. You can educate a client to expect the best, thus exposing the competition's weaknesses more subtly.

**Appearance and etiquette.** The way you look and act create a prospective client's first impression of your trustworthiness. When meeting a prospect for the first time, always dress conservatively (but never too formally if you know the prospect is very informal). Even if the client is dressed casually, conservative dress will demonstrate your respect for him or her.

Careful control of mannerisms is also important. Overtness and aggressiveness carried to the extreme can cause a negative impression. For example, when entering an office, always wait until you are asked to be seated. Avoid getting too personal immediately. Give the prospect a chance to feel comfortable with you before discussing hard issues. In other words, take as much time as possible to develop some rapport or trust before asking the client to rely on you for answers.

Once a relationship is established, you can expect it to last a national average of five years. To unseat the established competition, then, may require follow-up over a lengthy period. However, this statistic also means that at any time 20 percent of the market is dissatisfied with current relationships and ripe for targeting. If your firm is not the first to approach a prospect, assess carefully how much time you should spend on that company. Historically, if a competitor has already gained a high degree of trust, it is unlikely that a Johnny-come-lately will unseat or displace that firm.

## Suggestions for providing good service

Many technically driven design firms have erroneously staked their futures on providing the finest or best design in a geographic area or building type. Unfortunately for them, design buyers often do not look for the highest-quality design and rarely choose a design firm purely on its design history. Rather, most design buyers believe service is more important than product.

Research has shown that firms that produce a good product and have excellent service retain their clients better than firms that offer a high quality product but only mediocre service. Perversely, clients bond better with design firms after a mistake has been made and serviced well than with firms that have made no mistakes at all. Although this seems strange, and certainly intentional mistakes should not be part of any marketing plan, it is easy to understand that excellent response reduces the anxiety of the buyer, who then knows that any rough edges in the future will be smoothed out quickly.

For one-time or new clients, it is still important to emphasize the quality of the final product. These clients often have not yet experienced the problems of mediocre or poor service. However, as the relationship progresses and more jobs are contracted with the same client, research indicates that the service aspect increasingly becomes the client's predominant concern.

What then should project managers emphasize in terms of quality? The answer here is not so simple. It is apparent that many firms are incorporating too much unappreciated quality in their projects. In turn, they often become fat at the client's expense because of their inability to be lean in their product and pricing.

Carefully scrutinize each project and decide what is absolutely essential. What was a good thing to add for one client may be extraneous and costly for another. For example, a survey of one transportation engineering firm's clients revealed that although their state transportation clients loved them, more than half of their local municipalities thought they "over-designed." It is interesting to note that even though the firms studied had many client relationships that had evolved and deepened over time, their failure to maintain communication about client needs and the firm's response to them often caused these relationships to falter.

Further problems develop when design firms change markets without changing their approach to the jobs. For example, many architecture firms that have worked heavily in the hospital market have suffered greatly working in the leaner developer market. It is important to evaluate what is essential and what is unnecessary for each client on a continuing basis.

To keep growing and maintain the old entrepreneurial profit margins, firms must learn to stay lean, providing a high-quality product but not one that is more than the client needs or wants. In addition, good service must back up design work if you want to keep your firm's best clients.

# 2

◆◆◆◆◆◆◆◆◆◆◆◆◆◆

# MARKETING
# PLANNING

Simply put, marketing planning is a series of steps that allows a company to target particular markets and decision-makers. It attempts to provide a means of attacking these markets better than the competition can. Further, the process involves consistently evaluating goals, targets, and strategies to determine when revision is necessary and how improvements can be made.

Although marketing can be defined very broadly, too many firms take the narrow view that it involves only calls on new prospects and old clients; contacts with broad, unfocused networks of people who provide leads; and preparation and distribution of brochures, letters, and qualification statements. Although these are all part of the process, your marketing program will be more effective if you implement a broader, more comprehensive, and less risky set of actions that are focused by the first step of the process—marketing planning.

A fully developed marketing plan answers these important questions: Who are we? Why are we here? How do we compare to the competition? What and where do we want to be in the future? What rate of growth or profitability should we aim for? Which markets and potential clients should we target? What are the major strategies we could use to attack the opportunities? How can we assess the validity of these strategies? What kinds of tactics would be effective? How can we sell to and close the targeted prospects? How can we best service our clients? How are we doing, and can we do even better?

## Marketing services, not products

Because marketing is such a broad term it is important to recognize that design firm marketing is different in specific, critical ways from ordinary consumer marketing, to which we are constantly exposed. Most of these differences result from the fact that what is being sold is a service rather than a product.

Marketing products is significantly different from marketing services. The sale of products such as bricks or lumber depends on value (benefits and features) that can be seen and touched. The sale of services not yet performed (such as architecture or civil engineering) requires considerable advance explanation from the seller and trust from the buyer. The difference between marketing products and marketing services often creates confusion for design firms marketing a service that ends in a product, such as a building, road, electrical system, or site plan.

In fact, documented research indicates that design buyers depend on the honesty and integrity of the design firm to ensure that service is rendered on time, within budget, and with an acceptable degree of quality. The structure or site marketed is only an idea, so buyers must feel they can count on the design firm to deliver good service and a satisfactory final product.

Contrary to a commonly held assertion, design firms cannot create this trust and sell their services simply by showing a picture, or giving a tour, of a previous project. This effort, although useful, falls short of marketing the services performed and of answering the potential buyer's questions: Was the project completed on time? How many change orders were necessary? Was it done within budget? Were you in close, immediate contact with the client throughout the project? How quickly were problems handled during construction? Clients are concerned about these factors at least as much as they are about the final product.

To address these client concerns about service, your marketing program must emphasize the establishment of trust and must demonstrate skill, integrity, responsibility, competence, and dependability just as much as the firm's ability to produce the project.

---

## The ten steps of marketing planning

Marketing planning consists of long-term strategic and short-term tactical planning. It is a step-by-step process that charts the marketing course of your design firm based on present and future, internal and external conditions. It produces a flexible written document that specifically sets out what needs to be done over a three-year period.

The planning process begins with a series of questions: What is your company? What is its future? What kind of pace and scope will it take to reach that future? The ten steps outlined here will help you answer these questions and respond to and act on their answers:

1. **Determine the company mission.** The mission or purpose statement should reflect why your company is in business, give basic guidelines for further planning, and establish broad parameters for the future. This step is discussed in detail later in this chapter. It is important to start the planning process by defining a mission. This statement creates the motivational image of what type of company your president or management group would like your firm to become in the next five to ten years. It is the one step in marketing planning that involves looking beyond three years to the longer term.

---

### Using Outside People to Help You Plan

Outside businesspeople with overall knowledge of the company and what it is trying to accomplish can sometimes be helpful. You can bring in marketing people and presidents of noncompeting firms knowledgeable about the design and construction market at different points in the planning process to unlock difficult areas with an objective perspective. Consider hiring a professional planning facilitator to conduct the planning process.

**2. Set company goals.** Goals define the overall results your company wants to achieve. Write them in a way that helps your firm adhere to the mission statement and provides a foundation for the marketing process. Your goals should guide the marketing plan and the strategies needed to implement it. Goal-setting should begin with research—take a look at the capabilities of both your company and the competition and at what is happening in the marketplace. You can modify goals based on future research or, if you feel you don't have enough information to begin the process, you can perform a situation analysis before setting company goals.

**3. Perform internal analysis.** With goals and specific targets set, it is time to analyze the strengths and weaknesses of your company—what needs changing and what needs marketing emphasis. This analysis should include a client and firm view of your company's performance, including its previous successes in achieving sales and profits. Taking a measure of the company's position in its existing marketplaces will give you an objective feel for its strengths as well as its weaknesses.

**4. Perform external analysis.** An external analysis examines trends in the marketplace: hot versus cold markets, the local economic outlook, market types, available financing, and market needs. When performing an external analysis in the up-and-down, cyclical construction arena, it is important to research basic factors that can create or eliminate a marketplace for a design firm. These factors include the competition; economic, social, and political changes in the marketplace; and the need for particular infrastructures, facilities, and design services.

**5. Establish marketing goals.** Marketing goals should reflect what your company thinks it can accomplish through marketing in the coming years—for example, the amount of new business versus old, job and client profiles, and promotional and sales goals. Marketing targets and strategies are developed from the marketing goals, which determine the use of resources and set expectations for performance.

**6. Generate strategies to accomplish these goals.** The most creative and challenging part of the planning process is the generation of marketing strategies designed to accomplish your goals. Strategies are specific activities that can achieve stated marketing goals over the next two to three years. They range from pursuing a new type of client to expanding an existing market geographically or even changing your company's specialty. Strategies based on information from both internal and external analyses will serve your company best.

**7. Research and refine strategies.** It is important to narrow your company's focus as much as possible to one or two major strategies that will make it possible to reach your goals. To help choose these strategies from those developed, research the cost and resources required to pursue each approach and the possible obstacles to its success. Select several strategies that appear valid and only then move on to the next step. Caution at this point will save your company both time and money.

**8. Create and refine promotional and sales tactics.** Promotional and sales tactics are short-term, immediate, planned actions undertaken to implement strategies. Tactics should be specific reactions to research. For example, if research indicates a labor shortage, promote your company's ability to meet schedules.

During the promotion and sales stage, limit tactics to those necessary to accomplish marketing goals. Avoid wasting money by promoting and selling outside your defined goals.

**9. Implement the plan.** Once the marketing plan is put into action, good coordination and record-keeping are critical to making it succeed. Hold regularly scheduled meetings to review, evaluate, and suggest changes. The marketing process is flexible and should be changed to meet new circumstances as they arise.

**10. Evaluate the plan in action.** Finally, the entire marketing planning process must be continuously evaluated and updated. Conduct quarterly evaluations of your efforts to achieve your marketing goals, studying both successes and problems. This review will give you an opportunity to determine what is working and what is not, what could be improved, and what changes in the present and future marketplace will need attention. In addition, review the plan in terms of definite timetables, individual responsibility, and cost-benefit analysis.

---

## Increasing your chances for marketing success

If your marketing plan matches your firm's goals with the potential opportunities or needs in the marketplace, it can help your firm do the following:

**Produce higher profitability.** A marketing plan helps focus a firm's resources on the most profitable potential markets or clients, which can significantly increase the firm's profitability. For instance, clients that provide repeat work increase the business base, while reducing the cost of marketing competitively to attract new clients. Increasing your firm's sensitivity to a particular client through repeat work also makes it possible for you to render services to that firm more efficiently and profitably. In another scenario, your firm could target only corporate high-tech jobs where margins of profit tend to be higher. If many such jobs were targeted, familiarity with key issues of high-tech work would increase your firm's efficiency in marketing and project management.

**Increase organizational efficiency.** Marketing planning encourages a company to think about such issues as growth financing, financial planning, personnel planning, and bonding. Knowing what work is being targeted and pursued gives company leadership the chance to make educated financial and personnel decisions.

**Focus resources efficiently.** Marketing planning maximizes return on investment by allowing a company to concentrate its resources on the prospects that have the greatest potential in a given market.

**Reduce wasteful tangents.** In setting directions, marketing planning reduces the distractions that pop up and pull a company away from its optimal path.

**Maximize company potential.** Making best use of a firm's talents is critical. Design firm principals often get so tangled in day-to-day problems that the best possibilities for group and personal satisfaction in the future are lost. Planning forces executives to look at future opportunities and determine the firm's ideal focus.

**Reduce day-to-day problems.** To plan is to think about problems before they occur. Planning forces the company to seek the best possible course of action, implement a positive approach, evaluate and adjust this as necessary, and prepare for the next year. For example, if your company targeted shopping center development but had difficulty executing such projects at low enough cost, it would have a year to concentrate on recruiting less expensive subcontractors.

**Limit crises.** Good marketing planning reduces confusion and last-minute improvisation. Without planning, it is difficult to establish which problems your company should try to solve in advance. By identifying and limiting the types of problems a firm has with a particular market or client type, it is possible to attack and solve them in advance.

**Improve company reaction to downturns.** Marketing planning in the cyclical design and construction business helps a firm respond more quickly to unexpected changes. This is because good planning forces the leadership of a company to assess, through research, the possibilities and dangers of implementing a particular strategy. This knowledge suggests a need for insurance or contingency plans in case the primary strategy doesn't work. Also, if research is continually conducted throughout the year, it should warn of potential downturns, giving the firm more time to make needed changes in its marketing strategies.

**Make the firm more competitive.** Firms with successfully implemented marketing plans are more confident and aggressive in pursuing potential clients because they know where they are and where they are going. A focused marketing plan usually makes a firm better able to deliver its services profitably. This, in turn, provides the confidence to create tactics that give the company a competitive advantage.

**Provide greater opportunities.** Because firms with good marketing plans concentrate on locating and responding to needs in the market, their chances of finding the most stimulating and most profitable opportunities are greater than those of a firm without a focus for its efforts. Marketing to a marketplace that has limited needs or no needs will reduce your firm's chances for success both in the short and long term. A good marketing plan still allows you to respond to sudden opportunities in the marketplace as long as they fit your overall plan. Marketing planning can offer enormous benefits to a design firm. To engage in marketing planning successfully, however, requires overcoming some obstacles:

- It takes time to develop and implement a plan.
- It takes discipline to move forward constantly, especially in areas of limited familiarity.
- It requires ongoing evaluation, which takes considerable objectivity.
- It sometimes appears restrictive, causing a firm to lose what might appear to be opportunities.
- It breaks the comfortable, old intuitive pattern of reacting to new situations. That these reservations are minor compared to the benefits of engaging in marketing planning will become clear in the following chapters. These will detail ways to develop, implement, and continue to make use of marketing planning.

---

## Involving your staff in the planning process

A key to successful marketing planning is participation by those for whom it is most vital—your staff members. Ask for employee input. In small firms the president or a principal often does most of the marketing planning. Delegating responsibilities to employees according to their abilities and availability can relieve this individual of the burden of doing all the research and developing all the answers.

When your firm makes its first attempt at marketing planning, set a motivational agenda and announce it ten days to two weeks in advance. The message can be communicated to staff members in a memo such as the one shown on page 24.

Key people such as project managers, project architects and engineers, and office staff managers should participate in the marketing planning process. However, it is best if the marketing principal or president assigns the tasks. This individual can look at the company's limited resources and select those people who have the time and desire to complete them.

The president or managing principal must use his or her best judgment, vision, and experience to select these participants. Listed here are some factors to consider:

**Motivation and involvement.** In order to motivate the people you will rely on to move the company into the future, it is important to have them identify with and participate in the planning process. This personal involvement creates a commitment to the plan. Even in the smallest companies this is very important.

**Capabilities.** The team responsible for carrying out the plan must be capable of actually doing it. Expecting too much when there is neither time nor money creates frustration and failure.

**Resource knowledge.** The group should know which resources—the time, money, and other commitments needed to implement a marketing plan—can and cannot be made available.

**Presidential leadership or participation.** The president must be involved in the planning process. However, if marketing is not his or her love and another, marketing-oriented individual is interested, that person should serve as the planning leader. Keep negative people or naysayers to a minimum in the planning group, as they tend to deflate possibilities and stall discussions. However, cautious reasoning is always helpful and balances untested optimism. This is not a "pie in the sky" process but one based on intuition, fact, and research. Don't eliminate any creative idea that could enhance your marketing goals until there is strong group logic against it or research proves the idea is unworkable. When choosing staff members to participate in the planning process, assess candidates for the following qualities:

- Objectivity
- Skill in asking questions
- Listening abilities
- Common sense
- Ability to make practical suggestions
- Ability to research clients, owners, and decision-makers in the market
- Vision of the future

Few people will have all of these skills. If you can stack your planning force with employees who offer as many of them as possible, you will get the best results.

## *Stimulating creative participation*

Effective chairmanship is essential to a productive planning process. Beyond this, some very basic techniques can improve participation in your planning effort:

- To encourage creativity from the group at any point in the planning process, hold brainstorming sessions, with no criticism or evaluation allowed in the early discussions.
- Make certain participants write down their suggestions or solutions before presenting them. This controls the long-winded folks who can make meetings go on too long.
- Don't worry about the subjectivity of certain solutions; research will determine the soundness of all suggestions.
- To achieve consensus, consider everyone's ideas, listen to them carefully, and do not denigrate them in any way. The leader should never act as a wet blanket, smothering other people's ideas.
- Offer thank you's and responses such as "My concerns with this idea are…" rather than "Why would you want to do that?" This low-key approach will significantly reduce the negative feelings engendered if a participant's ideas are not enthusiastically accepted.
- Interrupt discussion only to avoid redundancy, clarify issues, stop too many negative expressions, or refocus attention on the key issues when the group has gone off on a tangent.
- Allow absolutely no negative discussion during or after the presentation of a solution.
- Don't permit any crosstalk when someone is speaking.
- Plan thoroughly (within reason) and get people on board. The greater your support for the marketing process, the shorter and easier the implementation will be. Why? Because participants will identify with and understand why the company is traveling that path. The firm that does not spend enough time planning,

or that dictates its plan, will most often spend an enormous amount of time attempting to rationalize, educate, and bring staff members around to the company's way of thinking.

## Tips for effective decision-making

Being able to make good quick decisions is usually a feature of a person's personality. However, certain practices, if adopted, can make any decision-maker more effective:

- In order to assess how good a decision is, think about how it will affect at least five people. In order to make this work, imagine being inside the mind of one of these people and verbalize his or her response. Repeat the process for each of your chosen people. If, during this exercise, you are not confident of most of the imagined respondents' words and thoughts, the decision is probably premature. It might be helpful in this situation to talk with the five people directly.
- Some long-term problems can be solved over a period of time by using tangible reminders to prod yourself to think about them. One way this can be accomplished is by writing down problems (no more than two per month) and taping them to the telephone. Write them in the form of "How to's." When talking to someone who may have an answer, ask the "How to." Jotting the response down and filing it conveniently can result in a host of solutions you may not otherwise have thought of.
- Speak to your network or other people inside and outside the industry, such as trade association staff, clients, and friends. When you are not sure how to ask a question, humility goes a long way. Suggest that you hope this isn't presumptuous and you are not quite sure how to ask the question, but...
- One of the most effective tools for smaller firms is to have contact with a few architect/engineer "entrepreneurs" in similar situations across the country but with whom you do not compete. Call on them when a problem comes up, and solicit their responses. In return, encourage them to call you.

## Generating solutions using the roundtable method

The following problem-solving procedure can save considerable time and increase the quality of meeting discussion.

**Step 1** (creating solutions)
- The leader states the objective of the meeting.
- The leader states the problem saying, "We need to know **how to**...," and hands out a typed version of it.
- Other participants ask questions about the problem and write down related questions.

## Using Spare Time for Creative Thought

An effective way to use the time you spend driving to and from home and on business trips is to focus on one or two problems and play devil's advocate with your own suggested solutions. To help you remember your thoughts, repeat out loud each pro and con or jot down key phrases at stoplights.

Although using this time takes discipline, it usually produces significant results. Another way of recording good ideas is to have a pad by your bedside on which to write down significant thoughts as they occur.

◇ Keep the objective of each short trip (up to 30 minutes) limited to one or two problems that are solvable in that time frame.

◇ Consider using a tape recorder. This is an outstanding means of quickly recording your ideas. When you are driving away after a meeting, you can summarize key points while they are fresh in your mind. Most people fear the recorder because they don't feel they can dictate. However, it is better to have your ideas on tape than not at all and creating notes from the tape is a functional time saver.

Having to think about a concept from the beginning, at your desk, at prime time, is very costly. Grabbing your tape recorder in the car is an enormously efficient way of retaining the ideas you come up with in that more relaxed environment. If you are still uncomfortable with the instrument, remember that practice will improve your use of it.

◇ Get subordinates to tape client service, prospect, or sales reports for you. Listen to tapes on issues facing your clients or on selling and time management. Use headphone tape recorders on planes.

◇ When flying, take paperwork that is not critical, such as background reading, correspondence, or reports. On the way home, use the time to write follow-up reports and fill out expense forms.

- The leader records on a blackboard or large pad the major "how to" questions.
- Participants are asked to write down one "how to" **solution statement** for each of the questions and to describe what inspired them to think of those solutions. Go around the room until everyone's solutions have been written on the flip chart or blackboard.
- The leader asks if there are any other solutions or "how to" questions to consider.
- The group selects the three to five solutions that appear to be the most adaptable to the primary question.
- When participants are concerned about a proposed solution, they should be diplomatic. Each can

—state the solution in his or her own words to eliminate possible semantic problems.

—state what he or she likes about the solution to point out what part of the solution is good or valid.

—state, "I have a specific concern with..."; for example, "Can we afford to market out of town: All this new work needs an up-front investment."

**Step 2** (refining solutions)

- ◆ Participants write down solutions for each concern expressed about each strategy or tactic suggested in Step 1.
- ◆ The leader goes around the room and solicits these solutions.
- ◆ Participants state their concerns specifically and briefly explain why they feel this way.
- ◆ The group members, one by one, offer solutions to answer these new concerns.
- ◆ If a solution is not acceptable, participants are encouraged to suggest other solutions.
- ◆ Repeat the process for each solution of each problem.

Another step for improving the process of planning involves thinking through certain basic, logistical steps ahead of time. Call in the people who will plan, determine when and where to plan, and decide who will accomplish what. Educating participants about the planning process, assigning specific responsibilities, and scheduling time to plan will eliminate many future problems.

Principals of smaller companies, who have enormous responsibilities in all aspects of running their businesses, often find it a daunting task to break out of the mold and initiate the marketing planning process. Making time can be difficult, and this problem is often exacerbated by unfamiliarity with marketing principles. To overcome these obstacles, take the plunge and establish a meeting schedule for the marketing planning process, then stick to it.

Planning is a quiet, thoughtful activity that is carried out best with calm, uninterrupted discussion. Following these few tips will give your group the mental space needed for success:

- ◆ Schedule sessions away from the office.

- Limit each session to three hours.
- Optimally, start early in the morning.
- Meet on a weekly, monthly, or bimonthly basis.

The time required to develop a first draft plan will vary from firm to firm. Generally, if participants complete assignments between meetings, the first draft of a marketing plan will be complete after six to eight sessions. Every company is different: some take somewhat longer to complete a plan and others less time. The difference depends on how much new research has to be undertaken. In either case, the firm must make a strong commitment to set this planning time aside. After the plan has been implemented, a monthly or bimonthly meeting for review and evaluation should be sufficient. Marketing and operational meetings should occur weekly or as needed.

As outlined earlier in this chapter, the marketing planning process involves ten steps, each of which serves as a building block for the next. Put them all together and the parts reflect the total—who the company is, where it is going, and how it will get there. Start by establishing a solid base for your marketing efforts: Define the company's mission in a statement that is workable and clear. Follow this up with a series of company goals that are practical and aim where you want the firm to go.

## Taking the first steps

### Determining your firm's mission statement

A mission statement is a statement of purpose and a management tool against which the firm's existence is constantly measured. An effective statement motivates employees and gives them a sense of opportunity, understanding, and achievement. The statement itself can be based on two questions: What is our business? What should it be?

A firm's mission will evolve and change over the years and should be reviewed on a yearly basis to make certain it is still motivational and appropriate to the company. To develop an effective statement of purpose, take into account these aspects of the company: its unique capabilities, its resources, the environment in which it operates, its history, and the personal goals of the owners. It is helpful to discuss with key members of the firm what they would like to achieve and what they believe the firm's purpose is.

A mission statement could read something like this: "Fessler Architects intends to be the finest architect in the secondary schools market. We endeavor to build a level of excellence unsurpassed by any firm in our state. We are committed to offering the highest quality service and the most responsible and sensitive architecture the educational system can afford."

*Setting company goals*

Once your mission statement has been composed, set your company goals. Although they can be modified later on the basis of situational analysis and strategic research, setting goals for the company at the outset creates boundaries for your research and strategy development. When you set the company's basic goals, you must clearly recognize its limitations in terms of resources.

Company goals provide the foundation for marketing planning, giving direction and guidelines to marketing strategies. They answer the questions of what direction the marketing program should take and what specific results are expected. Goals should be

- individually achievable, but motivational.
- clearly and precisely expressed so they will be understood by all.
- specific, reflecting hard thought rather than "pie in the sky" hopes.
- short, to avoid shopping lists of goals that are impossible to achieve.

Think of your resources—time, money, people—and match them against each goal. Company goals can be divided into these categories:

- Profitability
- Gross sales
- Number of people/productivity
- Type of structure or nonstructure
- Geographic reach
- Type or level of services
- Pricing
- Market share

Below are sample goals for two architecture firms. Each shows in parentheses the category it illustrates. These examples show how simply stated goals can be.

Firm 1—

- Create a level of service that will be perceived as the fastest in our region (level of service).
- Develop a marketing program that attacks repeat negotiated developers who desire speed above all other things (type of client).
- Increase the inventory of economy hotels (type of structure).

Firm 2—

- Find more repeat corporate office clients and service them well (type of client).
- Expand into two cities in our region (geographic reach).
- Begin doing our own superior advocacy on rezoning larger jobs (type or level of service).

## Goal Statements to Avoid

Avoid shallow thoughts and dangerous generalizations like these:
- Our policy will be to lead the competition.
- Our suggestive advertising campaign will have a high impact through its intensive aggressiveness.
- We intend to build our market steadily.
- We will offer a better product.
- Our plan is to satisfy the client.
- We plan to penetrate the high-class market.
- We will develop a system for keeping tabs on sales.
- We will advertise on TV and radio and through newspapers.
- We must get our image into the public eye.
- We will wage a low-pressure campaign.
- Our ultimate goal is to increase profits.
- We will produce a different product.
- Our price will be fair.
- We will seek a reasonable profit.
- We will base our detailed plans on our market research.
- We must stimulate the client.
- Our plan will increase sales.

It is important to balance company goals. Although it is probably impossible to apply all of the tradeoffs listed below, it is likely some of them will appeal to your planning group, depending on how much information is available to them. Try to balance

- short-term profits against long-term growth.
- profit margins versus competition and the state of the economy.
- the risk of new efforts against the risk of staying with what you know.
- penetration of existing markets against development of new markets.
- low-risk related opportunities against high-risk, nonrelated new opportunities as a source of long-term growth.
- profit against nonprofit goals and responsibilities, such as improving the work environment.
- growth against stability.
- a "risk-free" environment against a high-risk environment. *

---

*Presented by Warren Friedman at the seminar "Developing Management Strategies for Short-Term Profits and Long-Term Growth," New York, September 30-October 1, 1969, sponsored by AMR International, Inc. From Warren Friedman, *Construction Marketing and Strategic Planning* (New York: McGraw-Hill, 1984), page 25.

Once your planning group has come up with a mission statement and company goals, it is time to research the company's position in the marketplace and the best ways of reaching these goals. Chapters 3 to 5 will outline the research, strategies, and tactics you can employ to set your company on the road to success.

# 3

◆◆◆◆◆◆◆◆◆◆◆◆◆◆

## Researching Your Situation and Setting Marketing Goals

Once you have defined your company's mission and goals, it is time to analyze its strengths and weaknesses and its position in the marketplace. With this data in hand, you can set marketing goals that will enable your firm to increase business in the markets that best match its abilities.

It is critical that you get an objective view of your firm from both your staff members' and your clients' perspectives. Without such an assessment, it is difficult to set marketing goals and have the marketing and operational team agree on what the company should emphasize. Situation analysis creates a foundation for the remainder of the marketing plan. It tells the participants in the planning process what they have to work with and what they should beware of.

## Finding out where you stand

Situation analysis is divided into two parts: Internal analysis begins with an introspective look at where the firm is now, how it is functioning in the marketplace, and what its strengths and weaknesses are. External analysis tries to understand the competition, the market trends the company is facing, and where the emerging, declining, and steady needs are in the marketplace.

Fundamentally, situation analysis asks these questions:
- Who are your clients, present and prospective?
- What are the main concerns, problems, and needs of these clients?
- What is unique about your company's ability to give these clients what they want?
- Where is the company now and where do you want it to be two years from now?
- What problems must be overcome to get there?
- Is the company capable of achieving its goals given the present economic climate and its location?
- Who are the company's major competitors and how do they compare in terms of pricing and quality of customer service? (Be objective; don't underestimate the competition.)

### A look inside

Internal analysis has three stages. It doesn't matter where you start, but because the client interviews will take the longest, it might be best to start with them.

Stage I, **client analysis survey.** Knowing your company's strengths and weaknesses will help you determine opportunities for growth and potential problems that may result. Outside opinions from clients can help you assess how long it will take your company to make needed improvements and to what degree that time frame will inhibit or restrict company resources for expansion.

The client survey is critical to getting an objective view of what clients think of your company. Be careful, however, that your client analysis doesn't become too structured, time-consuming, and difficult. A lengthy internal analysis can bog down your planning process. Field personnel generally know what a client thinks of their performance, good or bad, and some information can be gathered from them.

Firms often are not satisfied with the results of client analysis the first time they attempt one. If your budget allows for it, an outside market research firm experienced in the industry may save you time and money. They can perform the survey with minimum disruption to your time and cash flow, and the results will be more objective.

Outlined here is a sample, step-by-step plan for a client analysis survey suitable for smaller firms.

Step A, **telephone survey.** Call several past clients and ask for their help. You could say, "We're looking to improve our service and would appreciate it if you would take a few minutes to share your thoughts. After our brief conversation I'd like to send a follow-up questionnaire. Am I calling at a good time? If not, when could I call again?"

When the client agrees to talk with you, ask these questions:

- In the past how have we performed?
- What could we do to improve our services?
- What do you think is outstanding about our services?
- Is there any reason you would not use us in the future?
- Is there anything you will be doing over the next twelve months that we should be aware of?

In order to get good information, frequently make remarks like "Thank you, that is very helpful. Can you give me more detail?" Under no circumstances should you argue or defend your company.

These research calls can be made by various members of the planning team. At the first planning session, the principal in charge of the process can assign all or some of these tasks based on participants' individual talents.

Good questioners and listeners who have some degree of objectivity should be assigned oral interview tasks. Have them call three major current clients to ask about their perceptions of the company's strengths and weaknesses. Questions could be, "How are we doing?" "How can we improve our services?" "How do you view us compared to the competition?" Answers should be recorded as specifically as possible.

Also assign several employees to speak to three lost or past clients each. Have them ask, "How could we have improved our services?" "What could we have done better?"

Step B, **questionnaire.** At the end of the interview callers should thank the client and ask whether he or she would spend another few

## Client Evaluation

Instructions: Please rate all our work and our company objectively.
We certainly thank you for your time and thoughts.

| | Excellent | | | | Fair | | | | Very Poor | |
|---|---|---|---|---|---|---|---|---|---|---|
| | 10 | 9 | 8 | 7 | 6 | 5 | 4 | 3 | 2 | 1 |
| Responsiveness to clients | | | | | | | | | | |
| Within budget | | | | | | | | | | |
| On time | | | | | | | | | | |
| Quality of work | | | | | | | | | | |
| Attitude toward service | | | | | | | | | | |
| Communications with client | | | | | | | | | | |
| Productivity | | | | | | | | | | |
| Human relations skills | | | | | | | | | | |
| Teamwork with other consultants | | | | | | | | | | |
| Flexibility | | | | | | | | | | |
| Fair pricing | | | | | | | | | | |

minutes completing a client evaluation form on your firm's past services. If yes, mail the client a score sheet like the one shown on this page and a self-addressed, stamped envelope for its return. Include a short follow-up note thanking the client for his or her help. If you have the budget, consider sending a small gift (nuts, fruit, or plants).

Step C, **tabulating responses.** When half the client questionnaires have been returned, tally the responses and get averages for each key area. A minimum of ten responses is needed, but to get some statistical accuracy try for many more than that. If necessary, go back to three- to four-year-old clients and ask for their input.

Step D, **evaluation.** Don't worry about areas scored from 8 to 10 on the questionnaire. Those marked from 5 to 7 need immediate attention and improving them should be part of the current year's

**Staff Evaluation**

Instructions: Please rate all our work and our company objectively.
We certainly thank you for your time and thoughts.

| | Excellent | | | | Fair | | | | Very Poor | |
|---|---|---|---|---|---|---|---|---|---|---|
| | 10 | 9 | 8 | 7 | 6 | 5 | 4 | 3 | 2 | 1 |
| Responsiveness to clients | | | | | | | | | | |
| Within budget | | | | | | | | | | |
| On time | | | | | | | | | | |
| Quality of work | | | | | | | | | | |
| Attitude toward service | | | | | | | | | | |
| Communication with client | | | | | | | | | | |
| Internal communications | | | | | | | | | | |
| Productivity | | | | | | | | | | |
| Human relations skills | | | | | | | | | | |
| Internal teamwork | | | | | | | | | | |
| Internal flexibility | | | | | | | | | | |
| Fair pricing | | | | | | | | | | |

objectives. Scores between 1 and 5 probably present long-term problems that will need significant work. A two-year objective should be to address these.

Stage II, **staff evaluation.** Staff evaluations are powerful introspective tools. Using a questionnaire similar to that sent to clients (see this page), staff members can let planners know what they think is important and needs improvement. Their views balance the opinions of outsiders gleaned from the client survey.

Step A. Staff members complete the questionnaire in confidence, and only the president reviews the completed forms in person. The cover memo should emphasize the president's hope for

## Basic Sources of Information for External Analysis

- ◇ Architects
- ◇ Engineers
- ◇ Developers
- ◇ Real estate salespeople
- ◇ Regional planning boards
- ◇ Client trade association or periodical personnel
- ◇ Salespeople who sell to that marketplace
- ◇ Consultants active in that area
- ◇ Prospective clients
- ◇ Friends and acquaintances
- ◇ Other firms in noncompetitive areas
- ◇ Subcontractors
- ◇ Local journalists who write about the subject
- ◇ Industry analysts
- ◇ Stock brokerage national analysts (local people might have national analysts' names)

objectivity and helpful, constructive criticism. It should also stress that the company's plans for growth will be based on this introspective look.

Ask staff members to use their own experience in filling out the questionnaire. If they have no experience in a particular subject, they should skip that question and go on to the next one.

Step B. Tally the results of the staff questionnaire and evaluate them in the same way you did the client questionnaire.

Step C. Compare the results of the staff and client questionnaires for discrepancies and consistencies. Some scores may throw off the average, but to find the best ways to improve the company, use them all in compiling the results.

When reviewing the results of the staff questionnaires, keep your objectivity. The responses are opinions and not etched in stone, so don't become defensive. The best defense is a good offense: figure out how to avoid the problem again. Above all, never argue with the results. Honesty was requested and received. It would look very silly for you to say, "I didn't want that kind of honesty."

As part of the staff evaluation, the comptroller/bookkeeper and the president should establish which have been the firm's three most profitable jobs in the past and review in detail the marketing history of these projects. Identify the company's most successful marketing tactics to date. Why did they succeed? What can be repeated?

Stage III, **job, client, profit, and sales evaluations.** Six tests are discussed here. These operational and marketing evaluations look at

| Internal Evaluation Test #1 | | |
| --- | --- | --- |
| Size of Job vs Profitability | | |
| Instructions: Have the comptroller or president fill out the following. | | |
| Size of project ($) | Actual % of profit | Actual total profitability in $ |
| 0—20,000 | | |
| 20—50,000 | | |
| 50—75,000 | | |
| 75—100,000 | | |
| 100—150,000 | | |
| 150—250,000 | | |
| 250—500,000 | | |
| 500—1,000,000 | | |
| Over 1,000,000 | | |

what jobs the firm has brought in and how profitably they have been processed. Their purpose is to get a general feel for what staff members think the company's specific strengths and weaknesses are and how they would be affected by growth. Only staff with direct knowledge of the specific test area should participate.

Test 1, **size of job versus profitability.** This test (page 39) aims at determining the job size at which the company is most profitable. When other factors are equal, most design firms are more profitable handling one larger job than three smaller ones. Is this true for you?

Test 2, **client type versus profitability.** This test (page 40) examines the relationship between client type and total profits. Usually, design firms service one market type better than others. Is this true for you?

Test 3, **construction type versus profitability.** In this test (page 41) staff can look at what kind of work is most profitable. Again, many firms tend to perform much better in some areas than in others.

Test 4, **market base versus desirability analysis.** This chart (page 42) reviews the current base of repeat and referral clients compared to the amount of new business desired and what markets the new clients

| Internal Evaluation Test #2 | | |
| --- | --- | --- |
| Client Type vs Profitability | | |
| Instructions: Have the comptroller or president fill out the following. | | |
| Client type | Estimated % of profit | Estimated total profitability in $ |
| **Corporate** | | |
| Small | | |
| Entrepreneurial | | |
| Large | | |
| Fortune 500 | | |
| Industrial | | |
| **Developer** | | |
| Speculative | | |
| Owner | | |
| **Developer** | | |
| National | | |
| Regional | | |
| Local | | |
| **Schools** | | |
| Higher ed. | | |
| Elementary | | |
| Private | | |
| **Government** | | |
| Municipal | | |
| County | | |
| State | | |
| Federal | | |
| **Other** | | |
| | | |

should come from. It tells the company how much of a base it has and how much needs to be done in new business development in order to accomplish the goals.

Filling out the market base versus desirability analysis will show

◆ how strong the base is.

◆ where the firm is competitive.

◆ the level of resource commitment that will be necessary.

◆ how much new business is needed.

Test 5, **sales analysis.** Internal analysis involves reviewing the following relationships:

◆ Total targets versus closed contracts

| Internal Evaluation Test #3<br>Construction Type vs Profitability<br>Instructions: Have the comptroller or president fill out the following. | | |
|---|---|---|
| Construction type | Estimated % of profit | Estimated total profitability in $ |
| Industrial | | |
| Corporate | | |
| Developer | | |
| Office | | |
| Corporate | | |
| Developer | | |
| Education | | |
| Higher | | |
| Retail | | |
| Strip | | |
| Single | | |
| Major | | |
| Housing | | |
| Single | | |
| Multi-family | | |
| Hotel | | |
| Medical | | |
| Public | | |
| Federal | | |
| State | | |
| Local | | |
| Heavy/roads | | |
| Bridges/roads | | |
| Environment | | |
| Other | | |
| | | |

- Total visits versus closed contracts
- Total estimates versus closed contracts
- Estimated total marketing dollars (including time spent) versus closed contracts

Although there are no norms for these targets and estimates, you should see significant improvement in the number of contracts landed in the year following implementation of a new marketing plan. Each year these figures should continue to improve, although probably not at the same rate every year.

## Internal Evaluation Test #4

Market base vs Desirability

| Building or decision-maker type | Shopping center developer | | | |
|---|---|---|---|---|
| % current business gross | 40% | | | |
| % next year's business with little marketing effort | 40% | | | |
| Level of skill vs. competition | 5 | | | |
| Profitability | 4 | | | |
| Desire to be in this market | 5 | | | |
| Depth of need in the market over the next three years | 2 | | | |
| Commitment needed in terms of effort needed to market | 5 | | | |

5=Excellent
4=Very Good
3=Average
2=Poor
1=Very Poor

5=Little or none
4=Some
3=Moderate
2=Heavy
1=Very heavy

*A look around you*

External analysis includes looking at trends in the marketplace (needs, sudden downturns, growth potential) and what the competition is doing or might do. Considering these two factors in combination with the strengths and weaknesses of your company should give you a solid base from which to make sound decisions about strategy and direction. The following steps are involved in external analysis:

- Determine the objective of the analysis, including the need to ascertain the extent of this particular market; determine how much the market will grow; estimate how long this market growth will last.
- Compile a list of those who decide which design firm to hire.
- Identify the specific needs and concerns of these decision-makers.
- Find out what particular segments of the market are growing the fastest.
- If you find a trend or direction described by the experts, confirm it with other sources.
- Develop a network of people who understand the market and could provide more in-depth information when needed.
- Choose important lead questions and include them on a survey form with a blank half page for recording the respondents' answers. Keep a file handy for this project, and staple the list of questions to the inside of it for quick reference.
- The president or another principal should call these people and ask the questions. Get the source to be as quantitative as possible. For example, "How many square feet do you think will be needed?"
- Rate the answers to the questions on this scale:

---

### Best Sources of Information about Competitors

- ◇ Subcontractors
- ◇ Other mutual competitors
- ◇ Contractors, architects, engineers, geotechnical engineers
- ◇ Financial support—bankers, mortgage brokers
- ◇ Clients
- ◇ Mutual suppliers
- ◇ Help wanted ads
- ◇ Developers

A = an encouraging response
B = a lukewarm response
C = a discouraging response

Don't be afraid to add minuses and pluses to make your assessments more exact.

- ◆ After the first few interviews, add any questions they suggest. This will reduce the time needed to perform the analysis.
- ◆ Make certain the name of the interviewee, his or her title, company, and phone number are on each interview sheet.
- ◆ When you speak to someone who is cooperative and has excellent insight, ask him or her, "Is there anyone else who might have your level of insight?"

Analyzing the competition is also an important part of the external analysis. To have an effective marketing plan, you must assess your competition in the same way you assess your own company. What are their traditional goals, strengths, and weaknesses? Where have they been tough competition? Where have they been weak? A determination of the effects of old and new competition and of what these firms do well will temper or accelerate a decision to attack a particular marketplace.

The objectives of competitive analysis are to

- ◆ determine the strengths and weaknesses of the competition.

---

### External Analysis Survey Sample

Review the list of questions presented below and decide which ones are appropriate for each interviewee.

Mr. (or Ms.)_____, I need your help. I'm trying to make some decisions for my company on its_____ . With your experience, I hoped you could give me guidance on a few critical questions. It will take about six to ten minutes.

Am I calling at a convenient time? If not, I can call back at whatever time you suggest.

Do you see the (your choice) market growing in the long and short term?

What do you see as the major trends in this market? Are there any volatile or cyclical effects that could suddenly change things for the worse?

Could you identify for me the major companies/clients in the area?

What are the typical types of facilities you think these people will be building?

Who else do you think is very knowledgeable about the industry and could answer some of these questions?

Do you know where I can get a list of key decision-makers in your geographic or market area? (when relevant)

Do you see the market as steady or cyclical?

Do the industry and area look prosperous as a whole?

We do this kind of work. Do you feel there is a lot of competition?

---

Include your major current competitors as well as those you think will compete with your firm in the future.

- determine where your marketing pursuit would be most effective.
- expose competitors' internal weaknesses and determine whether particular markets and strategies make sense in light of these weaknesses.
- ascertain how much improvement is needed and what kinds of resources are required to beat the competition.

To assemble this information, you will need to perform some more research. First, debrief key staff members to find out what they know and what they could find out through their own networks. Then, speak to existing clients and ask them these questions: What made you select us? What is your image and impression of the competition? What do you think is outstanding about them?

Contact mutual sources of information. Look through your Rolodex and see who you are friendly with who is also knowledgeable about the competition—for example, bankers, real estate salespeople, potential clients—and ask them the same questions.

To build files on each competitor, get a copy of their brochure and see how they are promoting themselves and what they emphasize. (Ask a mutual friend to get the brochure, or ask the competition directly for one.) Analyze the competition for their strengths, weaknesses, marketing approach, preferred job size, types of jobs, history, and unique features.

When information and observations have been compiled about a competitor, write a simple two-page analysis and include it with the evaluation of the firm. You can use something like the competitor analysis chart illustrated on page 46.

Finding out where the competition is strong and weak should allow you to create a better marketing plan. Tailoring your attack to others' weaknesses can be critical to the success of your marketing effort.

## Developing marketing goals

Once you have completed internal and external analyses and studied their results, you are ready to set your firm's marketing goals. These should be based on the company goals and tempered with information from research about your firm and its situation in the marketplace. If the company goal is to enter a new market, the marketing goal should spell out which market is to be attacked and set a specific target for the level of penetration to be achieved.

Marketing goals must recognize the limitations of the firm's resources and the expectations of firm principals. They can always be modified later, once more in-depth research and experience are added

| Competitor Analysis Chart<br><br>Complete this chart over the next 3-6 months.<br>(for internal use only)* | Company A | Company B | Company C | Company D |
|---|---|---|---|---|
| On budget | | | | |
| On time | | | | |
| Client service attitude | | | | |
| Trustworthiness of personnel | | | | |
| Experience | | | | |
| Communication skills | | | | |
| Quality of design | | | | |
| Value for $'s spent | | | | |
| Change order prevention | | | | |
| Marketing & sales capability | | | | |
| General reputation | | | | |

to the information gathered during situational analysis.

Marketing goals are the foundation from which specific sales, promotional, and research goals can be set. They also help define which targets make sense. They answer questions of how much research, promotion, and sales the firm should engage in and what results should be expected. Setting unrealistic goals frustrates the marketing effort, which in turn could endanger your firm's health.

Marketing goals, like company goals, must be
- motivational, achievable, and challenging.
- expressed clearly, so they can be understood by non-marketing people.
- specific, well-thought-out ideas, rather than hopes.
- limited.

Avoid laundry lists of goals, and limit your company to a few achievable ones. It is better to add a new goal later than not to achieve those on your initial list because in your eagerness you overlooked a lack of resources, time, money, and staff.

Marketing goals can be broken down into three categories: sales, promotional, and research. Review the sample goals below with these categories in mind. First are three for a firm that specializes in water treatment plants.

- Negotiate with six new developers and close three jobs (sales).
- Develop a rapport with key state EPA regulators (promotional).
- Determine who in the state will be building private wastewater treatment plants and is open to a relationship with a new design firm outside the area (research).

The following marketing goals would be suitable for a firm interested in designing for large industrial firms:

- Attack six new industrial clients in the Springfield area by June (sales).
- Develop a network of architects and engineers who are selling to the key targeted industrial clients (sales).

The processes suggested in this chapter have been streamlined, and you will need to invest a lot of time and thought to make sure your final marketing plan will be of sufficient quality to help your firm. This care is particularly important in carrying out the research for situation analysis. Without these simple steps the final product would be based too much on intuition, which can lead you down the wrong road.

Nothing can be more debilitating to a firm than finding that the direction it has taken leads nowhere and that this waste of time and money could have been avoided had someone spent a day or two on the telephone. The direct and opportunity costs of doing too little research are too great to ignore. The marketing planning process requires you to do your homework. Ignoring it is forgetting the purpose of the process—to develop a workable marketing plan.

# 4

❖❖❖❖❖❖❖❖❖❖❖❖❖

## Developing
## Strategies
## to Meet
## Your
## Marketing
## Goals

Perhaps the most creative aspect of the marketing planning process is developing strategies. Marketing strategies can be defined as the planned use of company resources to achieve company goals in the long run. Because marketing strategies determine where the company will be in the short and long term, they often serve as the base for a company's operational, financial, and administrative strategies and plans.

Your objective in selecting marketing strategies is to choose only those your company needs for its growth and profitability. Look at all the possibilities and develop the best of those that focus on achieving your marketing goals. Operating with too many choices dilutes your resources and makes it harder to achieve company goals.

## Steps for determining potential strategies

Following these steps will help you select the strategies that make the most sense for your firm:

Step 1, **use the market rating chart on page 52**. There are many potential strategies a design firm can adopt, each of which implies the company has specific strengths that can be matched to specific researched needs in the market. Adapt this chart to fit your company's special skills.

Step 2, **write out each of the potential strategies.** Develop a list of strategies; screen out the obviously fatty, impractical, and inappropriate ones; and write the others on a blackboard or sheets from a large pad or prepare them as handouts.

Step 3, **apply each strategy practically.** Spell out the options involved in following each strategy. For example, if you select geographic expansion, list the different ways it can be achieved—where you want to expand, whether you will start a new office, if you will employ a traveling business developer or a sales office.

Step 4, **emphasize creativity.** Push for fresh approaches. For example, wouldn't working with a trade association attended by all your prospective clients be easier than hiring a new salesman and knocking on everyone's door?

With these steps in mind, look at basic strategies and consider when it is best to apply them, the rationale for using them, and what you should be cautious about in each case. Look at and learn from case studies of what other firms have done. Another element that can affect which strategies you choose is the relative ease of introducing those based on existing, trusting market relationships. In descending order, it is generally easiest to market

- existing services to existing clients.
- new services to existing clients.
- existing services to new clients.
- new services to new clients.

When you are considering a number of strategies, factor in where they fall on this list to help choose among them.

---

Studies Market Research Services performed from 1987 to 1990 show how a number of marketing strategies have worked for design firms. The case studies used to illustrate these different strategies are based on real situations, but names, locations, and some facts have been changed to protect the privacy of the firms involved and to make the point of the examples as clear as possible.

### Addition of new services

An add-on service is a new service that is a logical outgrowth of a client's purchasing pattern. Offer such an option when a client likes and trusts your firm and its work and would probably respond favorably to an enhancement in service. From the marketing perspective, you already have the bird in your hand; why not feed it? For example, you could add landscaping, mechanical, engineering, or other related skills to the services you provide.

**When.** An add-on service strategy should be launched to increase profitability and to maintain existing clients who might switch loyalties if your firm is slow or unimaginative in servicing their needs. Add-ons can also be used to capture new clients who are frustrated with architecture firms that do not offer engineering or other services and who desire more architectural control of the key elements of a project.

**Rationale.** Instituting an add-on service makes sense when some of these conditions apply:

- In adding the service, your firm will attain a year's goal or a significant increase in fees/sales.
- The add-ons will solidify your existing client base.
- Client/customer research has indicated a need or desire to see

---

### Four Strategic Tips for the Future

- ◇ Knowing your clients also means understanding their business.
- ◇ No two prospects will have identical demands. Clients will become more differentiated and decentralized.
- ◇ Trying to plan for more than three years will be increasingly difficult. Economic, social, and political events will move as fast as or faster than they did in the last decade.
- ◇ Flexibility and responsiveness to market changes will be the two rules of survival.

## Market Rating Chart

| | Markets | | |
|---|---|---|---|
| Rate 10 = Most desirable<br>Rate 1 = Least desirable | | | |
| 1. Historical steadiness/cyclical nature | | | |
| 2. Competition | | | |
| 3. Current saturation | | | |
| 4. Potential saturation | | | |
| 5. Decision-maker accessibility | | | |
| 6. Negotiated or invited bid potential | | | |
| 7. Historical profitability | | | |
| 8. Negative/positive legislation possibility | | | |
| 9. Perceived risk | | | |
| 10. Compatibility with current services | | | |
| 11. Stress in producing good services | | | |
| 12. Interruption of present activities | | | |
| 13. Past profitability | | | |
| 14. Future profitability | | | |
| 15. Putting capital to best use | | | |
| 16. Conflict with lifestyle and firm culture | | | |
| 17. Technical know-how | | | |
| 18. Familiarity with selling techniques | | | |
| 19. Knowledge of buying patterns | | | |
| 20. Depth of marketing experience | | | |
| 21. Service know-how | | | |

the add-on service/product, reducing the risk of failure.

◆ The firm has extensive market share or a solid core of existing clients.

◆ Your competition already provides the service and could significantly attack your base if you do not.

**Cautions.** Make sure the quality and service of this add-on do not disappoint the client or adding them could have a negative effect. The scope of the service must match what the clients need or have requested. Beware of offering a "general" add-on when the client wants a specific trade or specialist.

**Case study:** Glorden Architects, specialists in strip shopping centers, was losing work to the competition because they did not offer planning services. Research among clients indicated they were frustrated by Glorden's work pace and their communications, particularly the company's inability to provide quick definitive answers.

**Action:** Glorden recruited experienced talent to offer planning services.

**Results:** Glorden solidified their hold on existing clients while warding off the competition. The appeal of the firm's broadened service increased its client base by 30 percent in the first year. Gross fees went up 18 percent and gross profits an additional 15 percent.

## Addition of lead-in services

An in-depth analysis of cost, a search for suitable financing, a feasibility study of a particular project, or a planner to help accomplish any of these can be offered as a lead-in service. The availability of such a service captures a buyer's imagination, commitment, and recognition of your longer line of services. Offer it at a loss, break-even, or small or large profit. The idea is to create a feeling of tangible benefits and outstanding and unique expertise early in your prospects' decision-making cycle so they move logically to the next step of purchasing more comprehensive services from your firm.

**When.** A lead-in service strategy should be introduced when you want to bring more business to your firm's profitable core services. It is used to preempt the competition by getting to the client first.

Rationale. Introduce a lead-in service if the following are true:

◆ The service will enable you to achieve your year's goals or a significant part of them.

◆ It will generate profitable clients without significantly altering the basic service.

◆ Existing services are profitable and more clients are wanted.

◆ The service can generate a significant amount of trust.

◆ A clear tie-in exists between the lead-in service and the follow-up core service.

**Cautions.** Initiating a lead-in service normally requires significant planning as you have not offered it before and to some degree it is outside the capabilities of your existing operation. To serve its purpose, the service must be of obviously high caliber and priced flexibly, to accommodate different client types' very different expectations. For example, when the service is provided

- below cost, it must be clearly established that this is a "loss leader" for other services and intended to demonstrate, for example, our "great services."
- at cost, let the client know "We want to help but you may choose not to go ahead."
- at a fair price, it should be based on established client demand and the perceived value of the service.

**Case study:** Newton, Tate and Associates, a $4 million local architecture firm specializing in office buildings, office showrooms, and interior design, was losing key targeted clients and jobs to larger regional firms. Newton needed a way to preempt the competition and get to the best clients before they contacted these other firms.

**Action:** Newton developed a specialized space planning and educational program aimed at young developers with strong track records. They aggressively offered the program on a one-time/no cost basis.

**Result:** Three of the fourteen developers offered the service gave them one or more jobs within six months.

## Geographic expansion of services

A narrowly defined service offered from a central location can be marketed to a broader geographic area.

**When.** A vertical service strategy should be employed when the service involves enough technology or sophistication to make distant buyers see a unique opportunity to buy "out-of-town" expertise they feel is not available locally.

**Rationale.** Vertical expansion is best when

- your firm has a base of experience consistently deeper than that of potential competitors.
- it is clear to the buyers that they need your deeper expertise.
- a clear, broad need for this service exists in many geographic areas.
- your company recognizes it could implement a long-distance, narrowly defined market attack.
- middle managers in your firm want to grow but still need some technical support and guidance.

**Cautions.** Your company must establish its ability and track record in servicing long-distance clients, particularly the willingness of your key managers to travel to project sites. To offset the cost of long-distance selling, your marketing support functions for research/lead generation and public relations must be especially strong.

**Case study:** Gross and Associates had a strong health-care base, having done many renovations for two regional hospitals. They wanted to achieve more rapid, though still controlled, growth from their base of $7.5 million. Although relatively solid, the local market did not offer more of this type of work, which was the only unique experience the firm had locally.

**Action:** Gross carefully researched a 250-mile area, including cities they could fly to within one hour, for hospital renovation possibilities. The firm then renamed itself the Healthcare Design Group and began calling on thirteen hospitals that had building programs for the next two years.

**Result:** Within a year, Gross had captured five clients, creating an operational break-even point after only nine months. In the second year the firm began two major hospital expansions with a combined construction value of over $5.2 million.

## Geographic expansion of your offices

A decision to expand physically to a new location should be based on offering the same services from a new location that will reach a new group of clients. The new city or distant location should have a solid need for and offer a new base from which to market existing services.

**When.** Undertake geographic expansion when the potential for growth in your current market is limited by

- a leveling off of the need for your particular services.
- an increase in competition beyond area or market growth rate.
- a client's demand for a local office.
- a major increase in price resistance.
- a potential long-term downturn in the existing market.
- a local economy that has proved too cyclical or too dependent on a limited market base. Another reason for choosing geographic expansion could be the presence on your staff of managers with strong skills who want an opportunity for personal growth in a more independent atmosphere.

**Rationale.** Geographic expansion can be effective in the following situations:

- A long-term need for experience in the design service you want to offer has been documented in the new area.
- You are comfortable using the techniques for attacking a marketplace as the "new kid on the block."
- Your firm has a unique depth of expertise in the services to be offered or a competitively superior commitment to service, quality, or pricing.

◆ The new market offers insurance against a downturn in a current situation. Occasionally, geographic expansion is undertaken in a defensive posture to prevent a strong local or national competitor from gaining a regional foothold.

**Cautions.** To be successful in the new arena, your firm must offer a level of service and quality that is competitive or better. Offering services already offered by the locals will drain your firm's resources while you search for a niche. Before you begin your expansion, research and identify the special needs and concerns of the market and match them to your firm's experience, strengths, and resources. Opening a new office to service an initial client contract is often a mistake. It is significantly less risky—and in the long-term, more rewarding—to pursue a new location based on a preconceived plan, rather than reacting to a short- or mid-term opportunity.

**Case study.** The Lesner Group was a twenty-five-year-old engineering/architecture company with a $3 million volume of business in a midwestern city. The company was stuck in a no-growth, general local market and was losing its market share to the competition, which had more experience in the only growth sector in town—renovating old buildings.

**Action.** Based on research, Sandy Lesner identified several major potential clients in a growing city whose needs were being met by only the most general services. Backed by her firm's reputation for excellent service in the retail and housing markets, Lesner opened an office in that city and carefully focused on special client needs in the new location.

**Results.** By the first quarter of the second year the firm was working on two of the most profitable jobs in its history, with the potential for repeat business.

## Solidification of your client base

In a client-solidification strategy, you market to existing large clients to achieve a greater share of their work. You assume the clients are satisfied with the work your firm has done, although you may have only 20 percent of their business. Quite often companies are so consumed with new client development, they don't follow up on significant existing clients who could fulfill their growth goals. This is an especially appealing strategy because it does not require building new relationships as some degree of trust has already been established.

**When.** Client solidification is a conservative strategy that usually requires less marketing effort than other strategies. Based on existing profitable relationships, it is useful when your firm is seeking increases in revenue and profitability with a minimum investment of marketing resources.

**Rationale.** Solidification is a comparatively simple strategy used to get more work without extending the base of clients. It is usually employed when

- your existing base of clients is substantial.
- client satisfaction is high.
- your quality of work is not in danger of diminishing if more jobs are added.
- research shows your existing clients would be amenable to giving more work to your firm.

**Cautions.** Client solidification can be a risky strategy if it means putting all your firm's eggs in one or two baskets for an extended period. It can also make a small company too vulnerable to the demands of a single master. Although client solidification is appealing because little new business development is needed, the lack of effort required can lull your company into a false sense of security that may make new business development efforts lackadaisical.

**Case study.** AJS is a local $6 million planning and design group in a busy southern city. With staff members willing to travel, the company attracted business from the regional offices of some major national retail developers. One client was particularly impressed with some good business decisions AJS had helped them make and thought the firm's in-depth knowledge of their business was unusual. As a result, they viewed AJS as a problem-solver rather than a "technical" design support group. AJS wanted to use this reputation to help solidify their client base.

**Action.** The president of AJS interviewed decision-makers at five developer groups the firm already served. Initially all five were reluctant to give AJS any more work, but when pressed two of the five said they were willing to let AJS try a "bit" more.

**Result.** The company's business increased an average of 21 percent per year over the next three years with an absolutely minimal amount of marketing. Profitability was consistent with growth achieved with minimum waste from learning new business.

## Acquisition of new client types

Before adopting a strategy of acquiring new client types, consider the potential benefits of selling existing services to a new client.

**When.** Searching for new client types is important if your existing client base is being competitively attacked, is saturated, or offers little promise for growth. This strategy offers a simple means of extending your firm's base of business without changing its staff. The new client types chosen should allow you to take them on without a significant change in service attitudes and procedures.

**Rationale.** Adopting a new client type works best when

- your company is familiar with the client type from past work.
- definitive research proves your chosen client type exhibits a significant need for the services you offer.

**Cautions.** Adopting new client types sometimes requires a new kind of client relationship. Rarely can you do too much market research when trying to understand these new clients' attitudes. For this strategy to be successful, there must be a clearly perceived improvement in service, quality, or price to motivate new buyers to switch their loyalties. Offering another general service in an area where other generalists are entrenched is often a mistake. For a new service to be accepted, it must provide a unique and substantially perceived benefit to the new client types. Attacking the market in force without testing the premise of unique benefits is a common mistake.

**Case study.** D. Resnick Interiors had worked extensively for midsize corporations in its home southern city. The owner, Doris Resnick, felt the return on investment she was making in this market was diminishing.

**Action.** Resnick studied the commercial park developer market and decided to launch a program emphasizing her firm's in-depth understanding of the developers' clients—corporations. Her theory was that the firm's very professional service and jack rabbit response to clients would fit comfortably into this commercial developer segment. She attacked the new market, offering the firm's traditional services from a new angle.

**Results.** Resnick Interiors attracted another client type, which was likely to offer repeat business, and grew 22 percent in the year after this strategy was implemented.

## Adoption of a technological innovation

To be useful, an advance in your firm's technical capabilities must be one the market will perceive as a significant improvement in how the function is performed. An example could be integrating geographic information systems (GIS) with your CADD system for a specific client type and market.

**When.** This strategy is advantageous when it offers the existing client base and market a benefit that prospective clients clearly recognize in terms of value, price, speed, time, and longevity. The innovation must be powerful enough to be the reason most potential clients would choose your company.

**Rationale.** Technological innovations are best when

- the market has confirmed the need for the innovation or its result.

- the innovation itself offers a means of reaching the company's stated goals.
- the image and direct benefit created by the innovation reduce your prospects' sensitivity to price.

**Cautions.** A technological innovation is only a marketable tool when your firm's proprietary interest in it can be maintained and the competition cannot copy or improve on it. Research your proposed innovation to determine whether you can clearly demonstrate its direct benefits to the buyer. Make sure you can easily produce it to meet market demand. There is no point in launching a corporate marketing program based on a service only one person in the firm can produce.

To be saleable, the innovation should not be an operational one that only helps internally. It is hard to make it clear to the market how such internal changes affect clients and contribute to their bottom line or success.

A decision to market a technological innovation works best if the change fits within the normal scope of your company's services and reinforces existing markets without forcing you into new ones. Marketing new products and services to new markets creates two stresses, which most companies will have twice the difficulty overcoming. This is especially true when new plans are undertaken without first performing in-depth research.

**Case study.** BRJ Heritage Architects was a regional architecture firm with no marketing program. They decided to initiate one based on some research that indicated developers of condominiums along the Texas Gulf Coast were complaining about the inability of architects to complete projects on time.

**Action.** After closely examining the situation, principals at BRJ Heritage decided a CADD system would allow their company to perform some design work more quickly. The system would also allow clients to view the work in their offices via modem, reducing delays for client approval. Staff members carefully researched the developers who had voiced this complaint to find which of them liked the concept of using a modem, were willing to pay for the time savings, and had a good payment history. The firm then sent letters to these developers discussing ways to accelerate completion dates and offering its new program.

**Results.** In year one, BRJ Lloyd's revenue increases totaled more than $1 million—a 26 percent rise from previous years. The second and third years produced 32 percent and 21 percent increases, respectively. In addition, in the second year, profitability went up another 9 percent per job based on performance bonuses received for early completion.

## Development of new or improved marketing programs

This strategy involves creating a marketing component for a firm that has done little or no marketing.

**When.** For a firm inexperienced in marketing, it is probably best to begin with a marketing program designed to bring more business into the company's profitable core services. The goal is to get more business from new or existing clients without altering the service being offered. This approach is an obvious choice when your firm's marketing effort has not been competitive in the marketplace.

**Rationale.** An aggressively launched new or improved marketing program is a good tonic when

- demand for existing services has flattened out and more clients are needed.
- competition or the marketplace demands a response.
- your firm needs to eliminate a lot of less profitable walk-in clients.

**Cautions.** Before you begin any new marketing effort, do some research to make certain the direction in which the group would like to go is valid. Once this has been determined, make a clear commitment to try the program for two to three years. This much time is needed for the marketing program to be satisfactorily implemented and prove its value to the company.

In an atmosphere where there is no consensus, a marketing program is often ineffective. Marketing must be an agreed-upon function performed by those with marketing/sales talents. Beware of taking technically oriented individuals and asking them to become more concerned with marketing. Most of them will not have the personality, desire, or training to accomplish marketing tasks well. If possible, select those with friendly, outgoing personalities to develop and execute the program.

Make sure your firm does not abandon your current means of bringing in business until the success of the new program has been proven. Carrying on this dual effort will mean additional work, but a transition period is important until the new program takes hold and produces results.

**Case study.** Ritter Plotkin and Goldberg (RPG) was a $1 million local engineering firm dependent on five major industrial accounts for the majority of its work. RPG's sales had leveled off for the past three years. It was known only among its clients, and aggressive competition was pursuing some of these.

**Action.** The firm decided to build a marketing program aimed at its existing client type base. Research was performed to determine the major concerns of potential new clients. With the agreement of project managers, this research was followed by a promotional program that attacked these client needs with more commitment than the competition.

**Results.** Three major new clients were added in the first year, increasing the company's billings 27 percent. In year two, billings went up 26 percent and in year three, 32 percent.

## Inauguration of a generic market attack

A generic market attack involves using a commonly recognized superior service benefit to attack many potential markets and client types.

**When.** The assumption you make when choosing this broad brush approach is that your design firm can create a perception of value that will be very clearly and quickly understood in many markets. From the marketing perspective, this strategy is rarely applicable and particularly difficult to implement. However, it can offer a broad spectrum of potential marketing tactics.

A generic program can be launched in many markets when a common significant complaint or need can be identified. It can be augmented by new technology.

**Rationale.** A generic approach is best when
- the complaints in the market are very clear, commonly stated, and numerous.
- in-depth research shows that launching the approach will allow your firm to beat the competition consistently.
- the competition will not be able to respond until after your company has achieved a significant market lead and share.

**Cautions.** Before choosing this strategy, make certain the complaints in the market are significant enough for people to change their buying habits easily. Beware of offering something the competition can easily copy. All staff members should understand the nitty-gritty components that make your firm's services superior. This attention to detail must become a clear part of the corporate culture.

**Case study.** Rish Engineers was a local firm, but it had done some work outside the area for selected clients. With $13 million in volume, it followed the local economic ups and downs. The company was the fifth largest engineering firm in its area, but was indistinguishable from the competition. After looking at the firm's strengths, Rish management decided their scheduling and efficiency were a little faster than many of their competitors'.

**Action.** Rish felt that if they concentrated on speed, the firm could become the "fastest gun" in the region, offering a major improvement to a variety of client types who "wanted it done yesterday." The firm spent a year creating a delivery system that surpassed anything else offered in the area and aggressively marketed its promise to beat the competition's time frame.

Results. After four years, Rish was leading sales in its area, having grown 33 percent per year and taking in what it felt were the "cream jobs."

## Using market research to determine and validate strategies

Nothing is more important than doing the research necessary to determine your marketing strategies and to verify their validity. This strategic research can be performed through primary and secondary sources. Strategic research is also called research/lead generation because it often results in a list of likely prospects.

To address the problems of these prospects specifically, necessary to the vital task of establishing trust, requires research calls to key sources of market information and focused calls to potential clients in target markets. These sources supply information about the client, the marketplace, the competition, or your design firm itself. For design research, a large number of primary sources and a small number of secondary ones usually supply the most useful information.

Primary research in the target audience is a critical and often ignored part of the marketing process. Its goal is to target prospects and determine the validity of marketing strategies in a selected market. Discussion in person or by telephone survey is the least costly and most effective method for learning about trends and attitudes and generating leads. The process includes ascertaining potential clients' attitudes toward their last design firms and their intentions of building in the near future.

Assign a staff member or an experienced outside telephone research firm to call both clients and prospects to ask what they think about the level of service they have been receiving, their industry's future needs, and their buying procedures. In most instances more valid results will be obtained if a consultant calls clients. However, if you have an experienced telephone researcher on staff, making these calls in-house can be advantageous.

Primary market research is the insurance that can turn a good hunch into a solid strategy and prevent a seat-of-the-pants idea from becoming a bad strategy.

Basic secondary research involves gathering data broader in scope than that uncovered through primary research. This background information can be used to validate a particular strategy or tactic, to identify such concepts in the first place, and to identify prospects for primary research.

Unfortunately, most firms do not have staff members dedicated to performing market research. Some individuals, good listeners and avid readers who keep up with what's happening, may have a natural talent in this area. If your firm has employees of this sort, assign them

## Tips for Good Market Research

◇ **Define the information needed in question form.** Converting general thoughts to questions allows you to define more clearly the information you are seeking. It also gives staff specific questions to answer with their research, simplifying their task and making the data gathered easier to understand and evaluate.

◇ **Don't reinvent the wheel.** In most instances, someone else has already gathered information about the marketplace in which you are interested. Although your competitors probably won't share information, other resources can be tapped. You will find most people willing to share their data. A simple way to test this assumption is to look at someone who normally sells products and services to the same market and needs similar information in determining their marketing plan.

◇ **Conduct joint venture research.** Design firms often seek information that general contractors, other design professionals, writers, and trade associations need. Consider working with groups that have a specific shared need in the same market or market segment. Such cooperation can reduce expenses, save research time, and in some cases offer easier access to potential clients. This access can be critical, because approaching prospects through a trade association can significantly reduce their resistance to your offers of information.

◇ **Seek out the target's past problems.** Recognizing that the average decision-maker will not look for a new design firm unless he or she is dissatisfied with the old one, concentrate on asking subtle, indirect questions: "Can you tell me how design firms can improve their service to you?" "What improvements can be made in the things architects do for you?" A reply indicating dissatisfaction with the individual's current design supplier suggests the target is a good prospect.

◇ **Chase emotion.** When talking directly to potential clients, be empathetic to their concerns and complaints and seek out the details of situations about which they appear emotional. Emotion is evidenced on the phone by a raised voice and use of harsher words or, less obviously, by long pauses, calculated use of words, and a slight rise in intonation or tone.

the responsibility of supplying the marketing process with research. However, if your firm can afford it, it can be a good idea to have a professional supply this critical ingredient of the marketing process. An objective outsider can provide the perfect antidote to the subjective, narrowly focused internal view of those with no marketing training.

For a busy design firm trying to verify a strategy, a quick approach could be to identify and talk to enough prospects in a potential market to prove the validity of the strategy and, specifically, its ability to achieve the firm's marketing goals. For example, if the goal is to close six prospects planning to build new nursing homes, calls to twenty-four qualified prospects would probably provide sufficient validation. In order to find this group, you might have to survey an estimated 100 to 200 potential clients for their attitudes.* This quick-step process for performing marketing research is effective for researching and verifying a strategy as well as generating leads and promotional and sales follow-up.

## Combining intuition with market research to get ahead

Intuition can help you figure out your firm's direction, provided it is backed with solid market research. Although many people will tell you intuition is not a logical base for making decisions, in marketing planning it is a good place to start. The problem most businesspeople have with intuition is that conditioning or stubbornness prevents them from abandoning their ideas when these conflict with the facts. As long as you treat intuitive hunches as ideas that must be tested and researched rather than the final word on marketing planning, your potential for moving ahead is good.

Facts, as represented by market research, prove or disprove intuitive ideas. Consider these three cases:

---

* Research has shown that in the design market the average client stays with the same design firm for five years. This fits other research, which indicates that 20 percent of any group of design buyers are unhappy with the last design service they were offered. Therefore, if you have a list of five times the number of decision-makers you want to close, it is likely you could achieve your corporate goal because a closing ratio of 25 percent of the 20 percent who are unhappy is quite realistic.

## Look before you leap

An excellent engineering/land planning firm that had a good share of its market was being squeezed out. Smaller competitors could do the smaller jobs for less and still make money. Larger national and regional specialists with in-depth experience were beating the firm on the larger jobs.

    **Action**—After discussions with two knowledgeable architects and much hand-wringing, the firm decided to pursue larger shopping center projects.

    **Results**—Although it had committed considerable time and resources to the effort, the firm captured only one contract. Its sales leveled off in an otherwise good growth year for the industry.

    **Lesson**—Later research showed the firm had underestimated the ferocity of the competition in the shopping center market. A more suitable market for attack was parks and recreation, in which, interestingly enough, a local competitor had landed ten jobs in three years, doubling its volume. The firm adjusted and did fairly well the next year, but the wasted effort and loss of hundreds of thousands of dollars could have been avoided with a little research.

## Too little, too late

A successful small Wisconsin architecture firm needed to move away from the shrinking local private health care work that had been providing a third of his revenue.

    **Action**—Instinct told the president freestanding radiology or surgical clinics made an attractive target. For five months he chased hospitals, doctors, and other related sources of work in this area.

    **Result**—He came up completely empty-handed.

    **Lesson #1**—The president found the market too spread out geographically with too many one-time decision-makers, making them difficult to identify and hard to approach efficiently. In addition, the average job was smaller than the company's average had been the previous year.

    After nine months and at considerable cost, the firm had identified only two developers of medical buildings. After another four months, it won a single contract. Once that job was completed, the firm negotiated two others.

    **Lesson #2**—A little more research, done earlier, in addition to more careful thought, would have eliminated a lot of wasted time. Savings, according to the firm's president, would have been "three months of my time and the company's lost opportunity. What's that worth?"

*The success story*

In 1984 a small architecture firm in the South wanted to grow. Intuition told the president a successful experience with an unusually large church facility ($2.2 million) gave him a marketing advantage.

**Action**—His company called 100 churches and researched eighty-one decision-makers, more than a quarter of whom said they intended to build within the next three years. Of that group, thirteen felt their last experience with an architect had been a disappointment. The client attacked these specific complaints in a direct promotional campaign and followed up with a very soft-sell approach.

**Result**—In five months the firm's first invited bid in this new market was a winner. Within seven months the firm negotiated two more jobs, and within the year a total of five jobs had been added. In the second year, 40 percent of the firm's business came from churches. The president declares the research the firm undertook before entering this market was "the most cost-effective thing we have ever done."

In each of these cases, finding the facts was not easy. But, in retrospect, it was not difficult either. A little resourcefulness always goes a long way. To start, ask the question "Who else needs or wants the same kind of information I am looking for?" Most markets have many attackers. In the design markets, the obvious groups are contractors, architects, engineers, developers, government regulatory and planning bodies, real estate salespeople, and various trade associations. Find out who else is calling on the market you are interested in reaching. These are the people who will provide referrals and bits of information that will help prove the worth of a "hunch" about the direction your firm should go in.

Once you have chosen the strategies your firm will follow, it is time to determine how to implement them. Strategies are critical, but the tactics or short-term actions you use to accomplish them are just as important. These will be discussed in the next chapter.

# 5

♦♦♦♦♦♦♦♦♦♦♦♦♦♦

## Great Tactics that Will Help You Reach Your Goals

Tactics are short-term actions aimed at achieving your company's long-term strategies. To be effective, they must be firmly grounded in your company's marketing goals. Market research can be used to develop sales and promotional tactics to attack the markets specified by your firm's goals. Such tactical research is also called prospect qualification, as it often helps screen leads.

Primary research can help you determine which prospects will be exceedingly difficult or impossible to close. Eliminate companies satisfied with the service of their current design firms. There is no reason to waste corporate resources pursuing a competitor's satisfied client when it is significantly easier and more fruitful to pursue dissatisfied ones.

Your company can also use information culled from primary research to approach potential clients. Offer to explain the results of a survey you have performed. Sharing such information on a regular basis positions you as a firm well informed about your prospects and their problems and able to compete with companies that may have deeper experience in the market.

Once you have identified prospective clients that match your marketing goals, you must reach them. The tactics that will allow you to do this are sales, advertising, and public relations. Sales (sometimes called business development) involves contacting prospective clients directly to present your company's services and qualifications and to bring the client to contract. Advertising promotes services by emphasizing desirable qualities through paid media or events to get the attention of your selected market. Public relations is the creation of a positive image for your company through free publicity, work, and actions of the company or its employees. It offers specific information about your firm (past history and philosophy) and communicates its desired image to targeted prospective markets and clients. Included are such widely divergent actions as publicizing through the media, sponsoring events, writing letters, and joining trade associations or civic groups.

Design firms should use advertising and public relations to support their sales efforts, spending about 80 percent of their promotion dollars for sales and 20 percent for advertising and public relations. Design professionals sometimes find these proportions hard to swallow because image is important to them. However, their pool of potential clients is small and their needs are better served by selling directly to companies in that pool than by trying to reach a wider, less qualified market.

Sales or business development consists of the operations and activities involved in selling design services. Sometimes a broader view of sales is taken to include everything the firm does during a contract to establish an excellent relationship. Although this activity is commonly called client service or project management, in a very basic way it is a sales function. For our purposes, however, we'll use the original, more limited definition.

This chapter will deal with the sales process, including generating leads, setting goals, making the interview or sales call, and screening prospects. Advertising and public relations and how they can support the sales process will also be discussed.

---

Leads can be generated through advertising, public relations, networking, "knocking on doors," and market research. All these methods make sense in different areas at different times. Proactively, the most effective method, of course, is to have a network and a market research program that attacks prospective clients when they are first thinking about a project. In such activist lead generation, direct calls and proactive market research are aimed at targeted prospects.

There are many sources of leads. The easiest, of course, is your list of current and past clients. The second most common source is a network you develop of engineers, land planners, contractors, and real estate and financial people involved in the construction process. Other basic sources are trade associations, subcontractors, and your firm's own staff. The advertising and public relations your firm uses can, if targeted, generate many leads. Last but not least are leads that come from *Commerce Business Daily* and similar sources, although these will probably lead your firm only to highly competitive situations.

In today's business environment, it is a truism that employees in a successful company market the company whenever they are in contact with the public. For example, a strong argument can be made that communication with a client is a form of marketing for the client's next project. Likewise, relationships with other professional firms directly affect a company's public image. Leads can come from clients and contractors on the job if your staff remembers to treat everyone as a potential source.

Once your leads are in hand, it is critical for the salesperson to set goals. Just as your firm has company and marketing goals, you must also have sales goals, which should strictly reflect the marketing goals. For example, an architecture firm considering an attack on the hospital market would like to have three jobs at the end of the year. From experience the principals know the salesperson will have to visit at least fifteen prospects in order to close three. A simple goal, therefore, would be to visit five new prospects in month one. A longer range goal might be to reach seven potential clients who have not been approached before in the first three months.

In planning sales goals, it is helpful to see the sales process from your prospective client's point of view: It can be divided into three

**The sales process**

parts, each requiring a different set of sales actions.

**Interest**—At this point the buyer has indicated only a basic, uncommitted desire to hear more about your company and its services. Generally the buyer has not yet defined what he or she is looking for and has only the most general knowledge of what that will be.

**Response**—Try to narrow and identify the key elements in the buying decision. Questions such as these might help you learn more about the prospect's situation:

- What are your major concerns about working with an architect?
- What are your hopes in terms of timing and scheduling for your next project?
- Can you tell me the major concerns of others in your group who help make decisions?

**Desire**—The prospect has decided to look more closely at your company and wants to know how, specifically, you can provide the services desired. Although there is no commitment to buy at this point, you must present reasons why your work is better than the work of others. Value, price, and service are all factors to mention. Unfortunately, in many cases the buyer is not qualified to determine whether your company can provide the services needed, so it is up to you to screen the buyer and determine how far to carry your pursuit.

Some key decisions remain to be made at this stage. The prospect must choose whether to bid or negotiate, whether to use design/build, and when to have an architect join the team. Reaching the prospect while such questions are undecided allows your firm to have some influence on the final shape of the project.

**Response**—At this point your salesperson, you or someone else, must demonstrate that your firm is more committed to the concerns of the client than the competitors are. Emphasize your firm's unique capabilities in servicing specific needs of the client. Use your position as trusted supplier to encourage the prospect to negotiate with your firm or at least to limit the bidding to a select list.

**Commitment**—At this point the prospect has decided to go ahead and will soon commit to one architect or another. He or she is assembling a team and is ready to make a decision.

**Response**—Selling at this stage in the decision-making process means sifting through what the prospect has said in terms of his or her final concerns. Now is the time to ask questions such as "Can you tell me whether, at this point, you are uncomfortable with anything about our firm?" and "Can you tell me whether, at this point, there are any reasons you would not use our firm?"

In each of these sales or buying steps it is critical for you to understand how, why, and on what basis the prospective client makes his or her decision. The keys to understanding, of course, are listening and asking good questions. Systematically debrief prospects without making them feel interrogated, and determine at each step how far the prospect has gone toward commitment and what response you must make to be totally convincing.

## The interview or sales call

The sales call can be termed an interview to remind you that it should not begin as an out-and-out effort to sell the services of your company. Proceed more subtly, offering useful information to your prospective client from the beginning. To establish and maintain a healthy relationship, continue this effort indefinitely. Some gentle probing should reveal more about the prospect's needs and concerns. Finally, screen those you have interviewed, selecting those prospects with the most potential for your firm.

Make your first appointment an opportunity to offer technical advice to the prospective client and to help him or her in the decision-making process. Your objective for this meeting should be to establish trust. It is usually best to avoid statements like "We are here to show you what our firm can do."

Research has shown that the most successful initial interviews are based on mutual benefit gained from an interchange of information. When you plan the sales meeting, include something informative and invaluable to the prospective client (such as a relevant experience, recent research, or timely article). The information should be genuinely useful to the prospect and a practical display of your company's thoughtfulness and understanding of client problems. It should be a no-strings-attached exchange—brief and to the point.

Make only a very short presentation (two-minute maximum) introducing your company. Then aim some thoughtful questions at the prospective client's future, such as "Mr. Prospect, what concerns have you had in the past with architects?" or "As you look at potential projects, what factors do you see inhibiting successful completion and profitability on your part?" Make certain prospective clients know their answers will help you better understand the job they want done. Don't try to drag the information out and do assure the individual, when necessary, of confidentiality.

It is important in this first meeting to ascertain how the prospect will choose a design firm. What issues are critical? This in turn will assist you, the designer, in deciding if you want the company for a client. It is possible that, after all is said and done, it may not be a job or client you want.

After the first meeting, you can enhance your firm's overall image of trustworthiness through more efforts at providing information based on client needs. Now is the time to establish your relationship with the client. Selling is best accomplished by reaching prospective clients before they think about specific projects. The integration of good public relations with your early sales effort is critical to such effective proactive marketing.

*Screening prospects*

Nothing helps a salesperson more than talking to the right prospects at the right time with the right attitude. Talking to the wrong person at the wrong time with the wrong attitude can be a very serious and costly mistake. Understanding and using the screening process will help you avoid this problem.

Screening is critical, from the beginning of the sales process to the end. How many decision-makers are there? How immediate is the work? What is the long-term potential for repeat work with this client? Do they have the money? Is the project type historically profitable for your company? Other issues such as competition and the promotional value of doing the work are all critical concerns that must be addressed. The screening criteria form illustrated on page 82 aims at suggesting a rating system for potential prospects.

Included in the form are fundamental controversial questions that can be difficult to ask directly without making the prospect feel interrogated. Suggested below is phrasing that can soften your approach but still allow you to elicit needed information. Ask these questions in a market research type survey or have your business developer ask them during an early visit after rapport has been established.

**How many decision-makers are there?** Ask, "Can you tell me how many people will assist you in choosing the design firm you hire?" or "I can send you some information on some of these issues. How many copies will you need for other decision-makers?"

**What is the immediacy of the work?** Ask, "Given your druthers, when do you hope to break ground (or start a new project)?"

**What sort of potential is there for a long-term relationship?** Ask, "What is your hope for an ongoing relationship with a design firm in the short and long term?"

**Has financing been established?** Ask, "Can we help you find or evaluate some financial resources?"

**What stage of project development have you reached?** Ask, "What is your time frame for development (choosing the site, purchasing the property, obtaining the financing)?"

**What is our potential competition?** Ask, "Can you tell me how you will make a decision about whether to use our firm? How will you proceed from our interview?"

**What is your past record with other design firms?** Ask, "Can you tell me how many design firms you have worked with? Have you been satisfied with them?"

The answers to questions like these should help you determine which prospects are worth pursuing—those who will have work and who seem open to hiring a new design firm. Carefully tailored public relations and limited advertising programs can help you reach these worthwhile targets.

---

## Making use of advertising and public relations

This section aims to clarify the value of and the severe limitations in using advertising and public relations and to outline the approaches that offer design firms the biggest bang for a dollar.

In consumer marketing the goal of advertising is to create a broad awareness of a company and consumer desire for its products or services, often without the direct involvement of a salesman. The opposite is true in design firm marketing, where the major function of advertising is to support a limited direct sales effort. In fact, design marketing seldom employs significant advertising beyond brochures and some targeted direct mail. Rarely does display advertising in the general media make sense for a design firm, which targets 50 to 100 prospects a year rather than thousands. Trade journal advertising to specific decision-making groups, however, can produce some name recognition as well as some leads.

Public relations for design firms can include everything from newspaper publicity about who will design a particular structure to a self-published newsletter. The most effective public relations seems to be those communications with clients that give them brief, user-friendly bits of information that help them understand their problems and opportunities.

Certain significant variables affect decisions about your advertising and public relations programs. Some markets require much more advertising and public relations than others. Consider the following:

- The broader and more diverse the targeted markets and prospects, the higher the cost of promotion and public relations.
- The larger the number of targets, the higher the cost of advertising and public relations.
- The higher the degree of repeat work in the current base, the lower the cost of advertising and public relations.
- The greater the potential of repeat work from one client, the greater the potential for focusing advertising and public relations dollars on a limited group (often at considerable savings).

No matter what form of promotion you choose, one factor is critical to your success: Your promotional program must focus strictly on

## Misconceptions about Advertising and Public Relations

◇ "I need some advertising to generate leads." More often than not, this idea is a pipe dream. It is very expensive to generate design leads with traditional display advertising or mass mailing of brochures. "To the point" direct letters and well-conceived newsletters or position papers are much more cost-effective sources of leads.

To generate anything significant in the way of leads, mass promotional methods must be used in a marketplace with thousands of potential clients. For example, in direct mail a good campaign will generate responses from .5 to 2 percent of the targeted group. If you mailed 500 pieces you would be lucky to receive two to ten leads, and the possibility of closing these is less than 25 percent. Consumer advertising is not a good way for design firms to generate leads.

◇ "I need advertising to tell my story." Quite often architects feel it is essential to have their stories told before they arrive in a potential client's office. This is important for consumer products companies that must reach thousands of people and rarely have the dollars or wherewithal to contact consumers directly. Architects, on the other hand, have a limited audience and the luxury of selling directly and telling their stories in person. For design firms, then, the objective of advertising and public relations should be to support the sales effort by establishing a limited amount of name recognition, easing the way for the sales call.

◇ "I need to get the company name out there." For a design firm, general blitz or repetitive advertising is more often than not a gross failure. It will reach many more people than intended, cost far beyond what the company can afford, and be functionally irrelevant to the eventual sales effort because the public has forgotten the advertising or public relations message after a few weeks.

your marketing goals. Otherwise, what is normally a difficult-to-manage cost can become a runaway loss. Consider the folly of one architecture/engineering firm: Its stated goal was to attack the hospital market in a 100-mile radius, but it spent 40 percent of its advertising and promotional dollars having a local public relations agency put announcements in the paper and produce a locally targeted quarterly newsletter. Through these efforts they hoped to attract walk-in traffic. At the end of two years, only two small jobs, both unprofitable, had come from that large portion of the marketing budget.

The trick for any firm is to get the biggest bang for its limited promotional dollar. To do this, it is important to spend most of the money budgeted for promotion on comparatively few prospects. Mass marketing approaches are ill-advised, expensive, and unrewarding for the marketer attempting to reach a small audience. The best approach is to target your prospects and spend your limited budget wisely.

Two letters to a targeted prospect are usually more effective than ten expensive advertisements a potential client may never read in a trade journal. Spend money on specific targets with a rifle approach rather than on broad-brush advertising and public relations through announcements. For every dollar spent on advertising and news releases for general name recognition, five should be spent on reaching specific targets. This is especially true for smaller firms.

## Types of public relations

There are many types of public relations. Better known methods include the following:

**Publicity** includes releases to newspapers, trade periodicals, or other media. The major stumbling block to success in this area is the ability to offer information editors will find newsworthy. An effective way of checking this potential is to monitor the media you are interested in over a period of time to see what types of stories are broadcast or printed. It is also helpful to call appropriate media decision-makers and ask what sorts of stories they would consider newsworthy.

**General community affairs.** If targeted decision-makers will be attending particular community events, full or part sponsorship can effectively attract their notice. However, to have the greatest impact, choose events that will directly affect the decision-makers you intend to target in the immediate future. Less productive are events that few decision-makers will attend. Even if your company does not sponsor an event, attendance by principals or other staff can be a good public relations move.

**Public speaking/seminars.** When aimed at prospects your company has targeted for the short term, nothing is more effective than a talk by a staff member sharing expertise about solving relevant problems. Prospective clients can come away from such an event with an image of your company as well able to communicate and share information as well as expert in areas that directly affect them.

As an example, one architecture firm offered a hospital trade association a mini-seminar on how to make better use of their existing facilities and how to take plans for additional services off the drawing board and implement them. The hospital administrators who attended the program came away with considerable information, as well as an image of the firm's president as competent, reliable, and knowledgeable in hospital design. Rather than making thirty sales calls, the president was able to telephone the four or five individuals who mentioned projects at the seminar.

**Client trade association involvement.** Probably nothing is more effective in terms of public relations than actively participating in trade associations with potential clients. Hospitals, schools, shopping centers, bridges, prisons and jails, multifamily housing, and many other specialties all have specific trade associations that allow affiliate or general membership. Joining one of these groups and taking a leadership role in committees or the general membership is probably one of the most effective methods of capturing a marketplace.

To decide whether this tactic will work for your firm, think about all the affiliate members of a targeted trade association and how important it would be for you to know who they are. In design firm marketing, wouldn't it be effective to meet most of your prospects when they get together socially? This not only saves enormous sales time, but it is an efficient way to collect information about the industry your firm is pursuing. Insurance agents, accountants, and suppliers have historically used this method to create a positive image for themselves.

**Trade shows.** If many potential clients will see your booth at a particular event, participating in a trade association exhibition can make sense. However, because of the considerable expense of creating an exhibit and the speed with which viewers typically pass through, it is difficult to establish relationships at trade shows. Before you decide to use this type of promotion, investigate past shows, especially checking with past exhibitors for their impressions. As in other aspects of promotion, an exhibit must target markets identified in your marketing goals to be successful.

## Characteristics of effective public relations

Effective public relations emphasizes the following:

**Targeting.** The most effective public relations is targeted toward prospects in specific markets. For example, a design firm proficient in hospital design might target readers of hospital periodicals and members of the American Hospital Association.

**Trust.** Whatever kind of public relations you use, try to create an image of consistency, dependability, sensitivity, and expertise, in other words, of trustworthiness.

**Service.** Market Research Services' research shows that, out of every seven dissatisfied buyers of design services, six are most concerned with the level of service they received in their last venture. Thus, any public relations effort should promote an image of commitment to quality service.

**The winner/leader.** Good public relations should also aim to create an image of your company as a leader and winner in the marketplace. Prospective decision-makers want to feel comfortable and assured that they are not taking a high risk; they want to jump on a successful bandwagon.

**Communications.** Because most problems that generate a switch of loyalties are created by lack of communication, it is very important for you and other company representatives to be good listeners. The image of a responsive company that puts clients' needs first is one of the most successful for any service company.

**Focus.** Good public relations often focuses on one outstanding attribute of a firm. Attempting to say that you are the fastest, most responsive, and cheapest firm all at the same time is generally ineffective. Most prospects are more likely to remember dramatic emphasis on one particular trait.

## Tips for good advertising and public relations

The following tips will help you generate good advertising and public relations campaigns:

- To reach prospects in the Think Phase, emphasize your firm's dependability and indispensability on key issues.
- In developing materials for a bid marketplace, emphasize your firm's competitiveness in technical skills and your ability to meet schedules.
- Aim public relations and advertising at prospective clients who are dissatisfied with their current design services. Although research shows this is only about 20 percent of the market, these are the people most likely to respond favorably to your eventual sales effort.
- Use nontechnical language to address those prospects without a technical background. Even potential clients with technical know-how will respond to good basic language that emphasizes service and avoids jargon.
- Spend 80 percent of your advertising and promotional dollar on specific contributions to achieving your sales goals. For example, if the target is an audience of 50 developers, make certain 80 percent of your yearly promotional budget is directed toward those developers.
- Address brochures to the expectations of your prospective

clients. If a client uses fancier or slicker material, a stark-looking assemblage of materials might fail. A fancy cover with flexible inserts that effectively reflect your specific design skills often has more impact than pages of pictures.

♦ Whenever possible, let others do the talking for you. Use referrals and testimonials. Ask members of your current network to call prospects before sales calls are made. Such techniques are vastly more successful and trust-inspiring than tooting your own horn in a presentation.

## Cost-effective public relations tools

For smaller and even some larger firms, certain types of public relations can be exceedingly effective and not particularly expensive. Consider the following:

**Letters.** A letter that specifically shares bits and pieces of important information with a prospect without any expectation of return is an effective way of gaining name recognition and the image of a company that cares about its clients. These informative letters can be inexpensive but must be very carefully researched to make certain the information shared will be valuable to its recipient.

**Article enclosures.** Another technique for demonstrating that your company cares about a potential client's needs and interests is highlighting an article, whether or not the decision-maker is familiar with the publication. This is an effective way of showing you will give personal attention to the prospect's problems. The image of the publication the articles come from can add to the effect. For example, an article from a respected trade periodical in a market the client is involved with indicates your company is sophisticated and familiar with that particular market.

**Referrals.** Whether using an established old-boy network or a prospective client's former design supplier, an effective way of touching base with a new prospect is to have a referral. This eases your way in the door, establishes a degree of trust, and, if the source is someone the decision-maker especially respects, creates a powerful initial impression.

**Testimonials.** Nothing is quite as effective as having a testimonial on how your firm has handled a specific problem the prospect has experienced. For example, if the decision-maker is upset about the slowness of a previous architect, specific testimonials on your firm's timely work from a few past clients will be exceedingly effective. Testimonials from peers or other people respected by the decision-maker can also help create a positive image.

*Brochures, a necessity*

Most firms need a brochure. This is not because brochures are an effective means of selling the company, but because they effectively support sales and decision-makers expect to receive them. Most brochures do not sell but simply reassure the decision-maker the firm is one of substance. The following checklist suggests ways of using, without abusing, brochures.

Do's:

- Be specific in listing the types of experience you have in the client's building type.
- Make certain the cover is of fairly high quality so it will impress any decision-maker in a targeted group.
- Make certain the information is "user-friendly" or very simple to read.
- Develop a brochure that engenders trust and an image of substance. Emphasize your firm's commitment to service and to understanding the potential client's business. Make certain the tone is objective and presents the firm in a judicious manner.
- Use a brief cover letter that highlights relevant points of the brochure. For example, "Please note the shopping center pictured is one of thirty shopping centers we have done."
- Emphasize pictures that will not become outdated.
- Emphasize testimonials and lists of clients rather than hordes of expensive pictures. Pictures can become outdated and, if put in the fixed part of the brochure, make the whole piece lose credibility. A few pictures of bigger projects create a better image.
- Try to use the brochure after a sales call. It is inflexible and cannot represent your firm as accurately as a salesperson can. It can be presented at the end of the sales call or mailed after ward with a letter summarizing key points.
- Make sure the brochure reflects your company's marketing plans, goals, and focus. It should not present a total "history" of every project you have ever completed.
- If you have an advertising or public relations firm prepare your brochure, try to find one with experience in architecture, construction, or engineering firms.

Don'ts:

- Don't blindly mail out brochures to people who have not requested them or will not be doing projects of interest to you.
- Do not create a brochure that cannot be altered quickly. Expertise quantifiably stated (for example, 30 shopping centers) will be more effective than showing pictures of irrelevant project types.

## Newsletters, useful if properly prepared

Newsletters are a common and popular public relations tool that sometimes can serve as a good lead-generation technique. More often than not, however, they are misused and misapplied. The initial objective of a newsletter must be to motivate the audience to read the material. Since most newsletters fail in this, shorter position papers are often more effective.

In the mid to late 1980s, many design firms adopted the newsletter technique, causing an overabundance of reading material for the limited audience. To be more effective in the '90s, newsletters or position papers must be explicitly helpful to the reader. Avoid self-congratulatory announcements of finished projects. Make certain your targeted audience matches that of your marketing goals, and don't mail the newsletter to thousands who are not potential clients.

To provide information that can immediately help readers be more effective in their business, focus on single issues of vital interest to your particular audience. Talk to your existing clientele and find out what issues are important to them and what information they would find valuable. Because a newsletter has only a few seconds to grab attention, you must appeal immediately to the reader to prevent it from landing in the "to-be-read" file or, worse, in the trash. According to research, only 10 percent of the "to-be-read" file is ever actually looked at.

If you must include it, put the less appealing, more self-serving information on the flip side or page two of your newsletter. This will soften the self-promotional image that can initially turn off readers.

A good tip for the first issue of a new newsletter is to have a cover letter emphasizing the paper as a public service through which the firm is trying to share important information. After your firm has produced a few issues, you might enclose a response card offering more information about your firm and how it could help readers with specific issue information. This card could prove to be an effective tool for generating leads.

If you want to produce a newsletter to keep your firm's staff informed about what is happening, a low-quality, typed information piece will often suffice.

Below are some general do's and don'ts for producing newsletters:

- Have a carefully screened, targeted list of potential and existing clients.
- Make certain the information is relevant and current.
- Avoid the appearance of wordiness—no paragraphs should be longer than four lines.
- Consider using fancy computer graphics and making photo-

copies rather than typesetting and printing the newsletter. This will save time and money.

- Number the issues rather than dating them, so the letters won't seem out-of-date. Use them as a sales support tool.
- Mail first class so the stamp will draw special attention to items. This will increase costs but also increase readership as it will avoid the look of junk mail.
- If possible, don't send items of a personal nature such as invitations by bulk mail.

Architecture firms that understand the differences between marketing and selling and between selling services and selling products; that know how to establish trust and use supportive public relations and occasional advertising; and that use market research and lead generation skillfully will be able to attack their markets proactively. Firms with this stance will have significantly more success in the '90s.

# Screening Criteria Form

| Characteristic | Excellent = 5 | Above average = 4 |
|---|---|---|
| How many decision-makers are there? | One or two | Three on committee |
| How soon will they begin work? | Break ground within 6 months of selection | Break ground within 3 months of selection |
| What is the long-term relationship potential of this prospect? | Excellent, for many years | Possible next year |
| Has financing been established? | All set to go, money in bank or committed | Needs drawings to go to lender but has preliminary commitment |
| How profitable has this type of job been for our firm in the past? | In the past all have been profitable | Most have been profitable |
| What experience do the firm's principals have in this type of project? | Deep experience | Much experience |
| In what stage of development is this project? | Property on hand, financing secure, ready to go soon, but no firm selected | Property owned; need A/E soon; program being developed |
| How many potential competitors are there for this project? | No others being considered | One or two |
| What is the firm's experience with this type of project? | Many similar, recent projects; cookie cutterpotential | A few similar projects in recent past |
| What is the promotional value of doing this project? | National and local publicity; good political impact | Limited PR but good political move, maybe magazine |
| What experience does the prospect have with architecture firms? | Has used our firm before | Has used several firms, understands services |
| Is the prospect local or out-of-state? | Job and prospect are nearby | Job nearby but prospect out-of-town |
| How recession-proof is the work? | Very | Somewhat |
| What potential does this project have for attracting repeat work from the prospect? | Excellent | Good |

Comments:

Excellent =
Good =
Average =
Poor =

| Average = 3 | Below average = 2 | Poor = 1 | Points |
|---|---|---|---|
| Small committee (one time) | 2-step committee selection | Large committee, then political group | |
| Within a year | Sometime in future, not sure | No schedule talked about | |
| May be possible | None likely | None at all | |
| Good prospect but needs plans | Nothing done about financing, needs help | Knows nothing about financing | |
| Some have been profitable, some not | Most have not been profitable | All have been losers | |
| Some experience | Limited experience | No experience | |
| Site being considered, program being but no firm | No site but idea of program needs developed | No site, no program, only vague ideas | |
| Several but not sure who | A lot | National publicity | |
| A similar project in firm's history | No firm experience but key individual has some | None | |
| Local exposure, mostly newspaper | Functional but not noteworthy (renovations, additions, etc.) | Not interested in PR | |
| Has limited experience but realizes need | No experience, ornever satisfied | Hates all firms | |
| In state, or job nearby | Job and prospect out of state but within 1-day trip | Job and prospect 2-day trip or more | |
| Possibly | Infrequently | Not at all | |
| Average | Not much | Would be counterproductive | |

**How to use the chart:** To determine whether a prospect matches your company's skills, read each question and choose the answer that best reflects the situation. Enter the number of points in the far right column. Total the points to get the prospect's score.

    To interpret the score, determine the range of points that will establish whether a prospect offers your firm an excellent, good, average, or poor opportunity (maximum score = 70).

Score: _____

# 6

◆◆◆◆◆◆◆◆◆◆◆◆◆◆◆

## Implementing and Evaluating Your Marketing Plan

O nce you have completed your marketing plan and developed the strategies and tactics to carry it out, it's time to put all your work to the test. Although you may feel overwhelmed by the marketing changes that need to be made, relax and don't try to do everything at once. Give your firm plenty of time to change, and don't abandon your old way of acquiring jobs until the new system has proved successful.

To keep your new marketing plan functioning at its best, you will need to evaluate it periodically. This vigilance will allow you to get the most out of your plan by updating it to meet new circumstances as they arise.

## Starting to use your marketing plan

Implementing the strategies and tactics established by your new marketing plan will be easier if your staff members understand the changes and know what their roles will be. Commitment and perseverance on the part of all staff members combined with a good system for monitoring the transition will make the program succeed.

### Who is responsible for what

Someone in the organization must direct the overall marketing effort and have final responsibility for ensuring that the whole company participates in it responsibly. If possible, create a marketing committee composed of the participating principals, the support staff, and any marketing-oriented or business development associates. Make this committee responsible for directing the effort and getting results. Sometimes in smaller firms the committee consists only of the principal and his or her secretary. Larger firms may have a marketing coordinator or marketing secretary.

Whatever size your committee is, it should be assigned the following tasks, which are necessary for a smooth transition to the new marketing program:

- Establishment of monthly goals
- Quarterly review of goals
- Monthly analysis of all marketing efforts
- Scheduling of biweekly meetings to consider operational issues and to monitor, evaluate, and develop the follow-up of day-to-day marketing efforts

To make sure these tasks are executed, it must be clear which staff members have been assigned which responsibilities. To help you assign tasks, examples of the roles of principals, marketing directors, sales teams, and support staff are outlined here:

**Principals'** tasks and responsibilities in the marketing process include the following:

- Motivating the firm's marketing effort
- Serving on the long-term marketing planning committee
- Recruiting, training, organizing, and motivating personnel involved in sales
- Helping key staffers refine their daily routines
- Closing deals when a prospect is ready to make a decision
- Recommending pricing policy for major contracts
- Establishing yearly overall policies and controls that will maintain total marketing expenses at satisfactory ratios
- Representing the firm in public relations ventures

The **marketing director's** responsibilities include the following:

- Centralizing and supervising all of the firm's marketing efforts, except closing
- Directing the marketing planning committee
- Concentrating and developing the firm's sales management skills: setting objectives and goals, establishing policies
- Supervising marketing support staff members who perform market research/lead generation
- Identifying and defining sales opportunities
- Establishing sales projections and ensuring an orderly, profitable increase in sales to meet these
- Following up or assigning follow-up on all jobs done for new clients to thank them and ascertain their next work prospects
- Contacting or assigning another staffer to contact all major clients semiannually to determine whether they are satisfied with the firm and, if not, what changes need to be made
- Maintaining all documents and files pertaining to client contracts and sales statistics and preparing related reports as required
- Collecting data for market and competition analysis, compartive sales analysis, and forecasting
- Assigning staff to monitor all targeted trade associations, their seminars, periodicals, etc.
- Identifying new markets, products, services, and opportunities and preparing definitive strategic plans, including sales (new market capture) and profit projections, to attack them
- Defining and implementing market research studies to identify new projects, owners, or developers by profile
- Developing and budgeting for promotional literature and programs to support the sales effort, including advertising, trade shows, brochures, newsletters, etc.

**Sales teams** are the groups of people you have assigned to specific targets or markets based on their experience and expertise. Their tasks involve the following:

- Participating in the development of new contract forecasts and

profit plans and pertinent supporting budgets
- Developing specific sales plans for key prospects that will enable the firm to achieve its new contract forecasts
- Developing new-project opportunities by contacting prospects, presenting the company's capabilities, providing useful information that will establish the trustworthiness of the firm, answering objections, and bringing prospects to contract
- Coordinating client relations with key staff members
- Maintaining contact with past clients and following up with those recently acquired
- Preparing biweekly reports on subjects such as the probability of acquiring outstanding contracts and the analysis of lost contracts

**Marketing support staff members** should have these responsibilities:
- Maintaining marketing files and sales reminder systems that centralize information about prospects, current clients, and past clients
- Maintaining slide and photograph files of the firm's work
- Undertaking market research/lead generation
- Assisting with writing and coordinating proposals
- Helping to create public relations materials
- Producing internal reports, as requested
- Maintaining good relationships with the press

## Transition from the old to the new

Firms attempting to become more proactive will have to make some adjustments, particularly in the way they handle their research, sales, and promotions.

**Research.** Someone in your marketing group must supervise the market research your firm carries out, whether it is done by an outside firm or a staff person. This individual should also supervise the staff member you assign to follow up on leads to make sure the following questions are answered about each contact:
- What is the depth of potential of each lead? Who, what, when, where?
- What are the company's current attitudes ("hot buttons") regarding design firms?
- What are the prospect's short- and long-term design needs?
- What response on the part of your firm will initiate a healthy, trusting relationship?
- What factors regarding the prospect may present challenges to your firm?
- What factors about your firm may prevent the prospect from

choosing to do business with you?

- Should your firm invest time with this prospect?

**Promotion.** Brochures that brag about how wonderful your firm is will not fit into your proactive marketing plan. Write your promotional pieces so they encourage the establishment of trust and credibility before and during the sales effort. Promotional materials must be based on a targeted attack on the market, with lead generation and follow-up screening, and should emphasize the following:

- Provision of information that has specific value to the prospect and cannot be considered promotional
- Creation of a fruitful relationship with prospects that begins early in their planning processes
- Concentration on the personal issue of service, as well as the technical issues of design

Base short-, medium-, and long-term promotional (and sales) programs for interacting with prospects on the predicted length of their decision-making cycles. Emphasizing prospects' needs will let them know you heard what they had to say. The information you provide should have a hook to it that leads prospects to look for further promotional or sales interaction.

All information in promotional pieces should be short and snappy. Stress the benefits of your firm's talents and what others say about your work, rather than the features of the firm. Demonstrate the firm's expertise with testimonials, quotes, or case histories that clearly express personal experiences your clients have had with the firm.

**Sales.** As has been stressed, sales follow-up in proactive marketing is based on a selling approach that allows a firm to establish relationships with potential clients before they have settled on their next projects. The idea is to focus on the factors in the design process that most disturb your prospects, offering them unique, outstanding, and dramatic commitments to resolving these problems. Such a focused effort will probably be more time-consuming than your previous approach to prospective clients. However, in most instances you should be able to reduce the number of visits needed to secure a contract by the simple change from selling to establishing your firm's image as a trustworthy supplier of useful information.

To encourage the effort required, you can establish a monthly quota of leads to be followed up. Offer a bonus or other small reward to those who successfully bring a project to contract. Assign each lead to an individual, or team leader in a larger firm, to confirm that company's outstanding needs as identified by the research. Other team participants can perform this follow-up task if the team leader needs more time to fulfill the team's quota. The major goals of the first visit to a prospect are to confirm the "hot buttons," put the prospect on a follow-up track, and establish what will be needed in resources (who, what, why, when, and where) to bring the prospect to contract.

It is best if the person handling a prospective client is the same individual who will serve as project manager if you get the contract. Team selling should be flexible, allowing the team member most familiar with a client type to service those prospects.

It is important for members of the sales team to keep a high profile in the targeted market. Continue to educate your prospects, possibly through membership in relevant professional organizations or attendance at various seminars. Also important is the creation of a network of people who can give you ideas for following up on prospects' needs as well as information about the needs of the marketplace.

Each time you consider instituting a new strategy or tactic, be sure to determine whether it will help your firm meet your marketing goals. You can eliminate a lot of wasted time by not pursuing strategies and tactics that are unrelated to your efforts. Well-defined goals will outline the breadth and depth of the implementation necessary to achieve them.

## Evaluating your plan in action

Marketing plans are evolutionary rather than fixed documents, giving a firm the freedom to react to events. Because of this, it is critical for your firm to continually check the effectiveness of your plan. Evaluate it every quarter, and undertake a major rewrite once a year.

A workable evaluation program measures your firm's successes and failures in achieving the goals of the marketing plan. It also provides an opportunity to correct any problems or take advantage of any major opportunities that arise.

### Evaluating staff performance

The best way to motivate staff members who participate in the marketing effort is to establish their responsibility for results. The first step is to establish standards against which their results can be measured. These standards, which staff members should help determine, could be as simple as stating an acceptable number of leads followed up, sales calls made, proposals delivered, or dollars spent in comparison to the number of people reached.

Quarterly reports should show how much has been spent compared with the sales achieved. Generally, this review should be both quantitative and qualitative. Review the financial investment and return as well as the success of promotional and sales programs, strategies, and tactics. Compare these figures with your original goals, budget, and time frame to determine how effective the marketing plan has been in operation. At this point, make changes in strategy only if a major event has changed the group's mind.

Include top managers at the yearly evaluation meeting, where you will review the total program to see what major changes need to be made. Financially, you need to look at sales compared to the budget, whether growth or improved profitability has been achieved, and what the return on investment has been. These are very basic functions that must be monitored.

## Evaluating costs

The cost of marketing depends on how aggressively the program tries to develop new business. Marketing existing services to existing clients is not costly, while expanding geographically or attempting to attract many new clients obviously increases expenses. The rate of increase can range anywhere from 7 percent to 15 percent of total revenues, and there really is no definitive way to determine whether the expenditure is the right amount at any given time. If a company is in an aggressive mode, looking for significant growth, and in need of new clients each year, the costs of marketing can reach as high as 15 to 17 percent of gross revenue. On the other hand, if a firm has many existing clients who are naturally expanding and only has to achieve 15 percent of its revenues from new clients, the cost will be significantly lower, perhaps as low as 7 percent. These parameters may be significantly altered if a company attempts to penetrate a new market and must initially expend more to accomplish this.

## Evaluating the program

Each review of the marketing plan should ask some very fundamental questions about the effectiveness of your marketing research, marketing strategies and tactics, sales and promotion efforts, and customer service. In terms of marketing information and research, ask these fundamental questions every quarter:

- Are there any indicators of change that would seriously affect the strategies we have chosen?
- Have we received enough information to make decisions about altering our strategies and tactics?
- Do we know whether our competitors are making significant changes in their approaches to our clients?
- Has our image changed with our clients?
- Do we know the earliest decision-making points that potential clients are struggling with?
- Do our potential clients understand why we are special?
- Have we analyzed why we lost jobs in order to avoid similar situations in the future?

Ask the following questions about strategies and tactics:

- Is this strategy understandable and precise?
- Is this strategy based on irrefutable evidence of the competition's strengths and weaknesses? Do we have a program to overcome the former and exploit the latter?

Ask these basic questions about your sales program every quarter:

- Are we making enough sales calls to reach our goal?
- How many sales calls are we making per potential client and can we be more efficient?
- Is there any way to reduce the labor intensity of making sales calls to potential clients?
- Are we listening to the needs our clients express? Are these needs changing?
- Do our sales techniques reflect the type of client we are trying to close?
- Are we selling solutions or are we reactively selling ourselves?

In terms of promotion, the firm should ask these questions on a quarterly basis:

- Are our solutions and the information we share relevant to the clients' needs?
- Do the letters and other communication tools we use reflect the best of what we are?
- Have we, in our approach, differentiated ourselves from our competitors?
- Are we perceived as the expert by clients and prospects?
- Are we applying enough resources to accomplish our task?
- Are there situations in which we could reduce the number of resources by focusing our efforts better?
- Are we wasting resources on nonessential image-building when we could be more effective by targeting fewer clients and pouring more money into the effort of landing them?

To check the effectiveness of your customer service, ask this question every quarter:

- Are our clients satisfied and to what degree?

Although most firms feel they cannot afford the time needed to evaluate their marketing process extensively, those who spend the time get better results. Make certain, though, that you don't spend too much time on details and get bogged down in theoretical planning. There is nothing worse than inaction in the marketing arena. It is demoralizing and shuts off the fountain from which the firm will drink in the near future. Firms that take too long to make decisions and hesitate to implement proactive marketing plans will be left behind or lose significant opportunities in the 1990s.

# POSTSCRIPT

◆◆◆◆◆◆◆◆◆◆◆◆◆◆◆

# WHAT
# MARKETING
# WINNERS DO

Although every successful company does hundreds of special things in its marketing, certain fundamentals generally hold true:

◆ **Marketing winners practice the KISS method (Keep It Simple, Stupid).** Keeping things simple in a marketing program can be difficult. Strive to accomplish the following:

—*Reduce the number and type of special commitments to clients.* Avoid trying to be "all things to all clients." For example, a company is more likely to achieve the "speediest" delivery if it commits all its resources to this endeavor. Trying to offer precise pricing, few change orders, and high quality, all in the same year as fast delivery, will significantly reduce your chances for success.

—*Use language the client can clearly understand.* Replace designer jargon with simple explanations that squarely meet the client's level of sophistication.

—*Focus on basic benefits, such as saving time and money.*

—*Concentrate only on the prospective client's stated concerns and needs, and use customized letters to communicate your interest in these.* These practices allow design firms to offer an appropriate "rifle shot" response, which helps keep promotional costs reasonable.

◆ **Marketing winners are flexible.** To truly meet a client's needs, it is important for design firms to think of those needs rather than of fitting the client into the internal rules and policies of the firm. Gather information to determine whether your strategies and tactics are valid before they become part of the marketing plan. Be prepared to move from one focused target market to another in the event of a downturn.

◆ **Marketing winners solicit ongoing client feedback.** Tom Peters reported in his 1982 book, *In Search of Excellence: Lessons from America's Best Run Companies,* that one outstanding attribute of winning companies was their commitment to stay close to their clients. This simple rule can easily be followed by calling or writing current customers and asking, in the name of doing a better job, "How are we doing?" Contact can be made by your firm's principals in the form of a personal letter or a telephone call. The president can place a few phone calls during the course of a job, and the project manager can send a personal letter at its conclusion. The key is to show clients your firm is interested in them and their opinions and wants an objective analysis of how they are being served and how you could serve them better.

The objective of this book is to give architects who have never had formal training a marketing planning ability that will allow them to hurdle the obstacles of developing a marketing plan for the first time or take the plunge and improve on past efforts. If you want success—more work, a better mix of work, increased fees, and a consistent work load—it will take commitment and effort.

Thoughtful planning will help you build a marketing plan for your design firm and a solid base for your business. Take the step, and, to paraphrase Henry David Thoreau, "If you advance confidently in the direction of your dreams, and endeavor to live the life you have imagined, you will meet with a success unexpected in common hours."